Kalaripayat

Kalaripayat

The Martial Arts Tradition of India

Patrick Denaud

Translated by Jack Cain

Destiny Books

Rochester, Vermont • Toronto, Canada

Destiny Books
One Park Street
Rochester, Vermont 05767
www.DestinyBooks.com

Destiny Books is a division of Inner Traditions International

Originally published in French under the title *Kalaripayat: L'origine des arts martiaux* by Éditions Budostore
First U.S. edition published in 2009 by Destiny Books

Library of Congress Cataloging-in-Publication Data
Denaud, Patrick.
  Kalaripayat : the martial arts tradition of India / Patrick Denaud ; translated by Jack Cain.—1st u.s. ed.
     p. cm.
  "Originally published in French under the title Kalaripayat."
  Includes bibliographical references and index.
  Summary: "A definitive look at the most ancient of the Eastern martial arts."
  —Provided by the publisher.
  ISBN 978-1-59477-315-0 (pbk.)
  1. Martial arts—India. I. Title.
  GV1100.71.A2D46 2009
  796.80954—dc22

                                                    2009030075

Printed and bound in the United States by PA Hutchison

10   9   8   7   6   5   4   3   2   1

Text design by Jon Desautels
Text layout by Virginia Scott Bowman

This book was typeset in Garamond Premier Pro and Agenda with Poster Bodoni and Agenda Condensed as display typefaces

*We thank Master P. S. Balachandran and
the Indian School of Martial Arts.*

Contents

APPENDIX: WHERE TO PRACTICE   149

Acknowledgments

We thank Mr. Kanijilal, Mrs. Nalini Netto, Mr. Rao, and Mr. Shaw of the Office of Indian Tourism, without whom this book would never have seen the light of day. Thanks also to Martine Chemana and Liliane Tourtet.

Kalaripayat

Record and Portent

Kalaripayat—the first time Patrick Denaud spoke to me about his desire to write a book on this topic, my immediate reaction was to savor this delightful word. Kalaripayat—of no meaning to me, and yet conveying a special quality through its sound: a harmony, a powerful shape, a palpable force.

He spoke to me about it as a journalist would—a real journalist—with precision, clarity, directness, and enthusiasm. He told me the story of his trip, speaking of the people he had met, what he had experienced, and what he had seen. I reveled in having this far-flung province of Kerala penetrate into my modern Western world and in the radically new insights that our conversation brought to my meager knowledge of India.

India is very definitely one of our cultural "motherlands," as the Indo-European basis of our language makes clear. I have no doubt that this civilization occupies, often without our really being aware of it, a significant place in our collective memory.

As a practitioner of a martial art, I've always regretted having to look for the theoretical and philosophical foundations of my discipline deep within some other civilization. I never imagined that the foundation of the martial arts in Far-Eastern civilization could be found in an Indian tradition. As Patrick Denaud confidently makes clear, Kalaripayat arose in India prior to all other martial arts. From there, it spread out and influenced all subsequent practice—including that of China, Korea, and Japan!

There is something deeply magical about India. It has a complex subtlety (or a subtle complexity) and Kalaripayat is very much a part of that. It is an authentic and extremely rich martial art—which includes techniques, massage, meditation, medicine, and self-defense—yet at the same time it avoids the impulse toward confusion or mystification by being clear and simple. Kalaripayat is total, complete, and complex . . . but without complexes.

I am delighted to be the publisher of the first book in French on this topic. I am most particularly delighted in feeling that the modern world of martial arts is beginning to soar toward an era that seems more global, richer, and more full of possibilities. I am also pleased that Kalaripayat is not solely an art of the past, but rather an art of the present day; it is a record but at the same time a portent.

Thierry Plée
Publisher of the French edition

The Indian Legacy of Martial Arts

Through the richness of its culture and the antiquity of its civilization, India has for centuries attracted many travelers from the four corners of the earth. Some go to make their fortune, others to discover a country and its people, a culture, or a craft. Today, the main reasons that bring travelers to India are most often connected with tourism, but in India tourism often goes hand in hand with the discovery of—and then sometimes an immersion in—certain traditions whose origins are buried in the mists of time.

Kalaripayat is one such tradition. It is a martial art that originated in India, as did the martial arts of Vajra Musti and Varma Kalai. Although not as well known as yoga, dance, or music, Indian martial arts are nevertheless very much a part of India's cultural heritage. They are now emerging from a long period of neglect as they gradually regain their former honored status. Just as with yoga, Indian martial arts constitute a method of personal development designed to strengthen the body and to attain a harmony of mind and body with which to face life and its aggressions.

Kalaripayat is a complete discipline that combines physical

training, mental tasks, and self-discipline. It demands a knowledge of the body, of traditional Indian Ayurvedic medicine, and of the art of massage. As with all the other traditions in India, Kalaripayat is passed on today from master to pupil in the villages. Increasingly it is also attracting a significant number of foreign students who are looking for the real essence of Eastern martial arts.

Martial arts in India grew out of an observation of the animal kingdom in its natural environment; their practitioners are thus plunged into a deep communication with nature herself. According to tradition, Kerala residents owe this art to Parasurama, one of the avatars of Vishnu (one of India's three main gods). It is said that, after having rescued Kerala from sinking into the ocean, Parasurama taught this art to twenty-one disciples so that they could protect the country and keep it peaceful.

Primarily an art of self-defense, Kalaripayat is meant to bring inner calm to the practitioner who, in turn, will then be in a position to disseminate that state to those around. We commend Patrick Denaud's initiative in striving to bring to light one of the many misunderstood facets of Indian tradition. In this book he offers his readers—novices and specialists alike—a very complete overview of this art, which leads the practitioner to improved self-knowledge and a transformed view of others.

P. K. KAPUR
CULTURAL ATTACHÉ WITH THE INDIAN EMBASSY

The Noble Art of Kalaripayat

India, that vast Asian country with over a billion inhabitants, is the home of one of the most ancient Eastern martial arts: Kalaripayat.

Kalaripayat is not only a martial art; it is above all a state of mind, a way of life. It is a noble art that inevitably leads to purity of body and mind. It's a unity: control of the body must go hand in hand with mastery of the psyche in order to move toward spiritual perfection. The way is long and demands regular practice. Each element must be undertaken and learned at the right time, at the right moment. Steps cannot be skipped. "You must learn to walk before you learn to run."

Kalaripayat is based on a science of breathing, which is a very important aspect of the art. After years of practice, it allows control of the essential organs of the human body (such as heart, stomach, and kidneys), leading to a flexibility of body and mind. Deep and silent breathing can lead to a "state of ecstasy." The intended aim is the inner circulation of various vital essences. In a way it's life in a closed circuit. The techniques used are close to those used in yoga, and the practice of Kalaripayat allows one to enter into states that are favorable to meditation.

Kalaripayat is considered an instrument of spiritual attainment, but it is also related to Indian medicine. This makes sense because a human being is a unity—the body and soul are indivisible. And the soul cannot live in a body that is ill. Kalaripayat masters often heal using plants. Each master has his secrets that have been passed down from his ancestors and that he will transmit in his turn to his grandchildren.

Massage is also used a great deal to promote circulation of energy through the whole body and foster harmonious development of the individual. The study of pressure points is also part of the program for Kalaripayat practitioners.

Certain combat techniques are derived from the observation of animals in their respective natural habitats. These techniques are based on the stance and skills of these animals in defense and attack.

Kalaripayat is a physical discipline but a very spiritual one. This discipline demands rigor, order, and precision to a degree not found elsewhere. Arising first in India, Kalaripayat later influenced the martial arts practices of China and Japan in those places where spiritual influences prevailed.

Everyone respects the moral precepts conveyed by the master such as respect, politeness, humility, patience, self-control, and obedience. The practitioner must be an example for society and must come to the aid of others. For us, as Westerners, there are great difficulties in understanding all the subtleties of this art, since we don't really grasp Eastern spirituality. However, the moral riches of Kalaripayat can bring a great deal to this world modern humanity has created—a chiefly material setting based on ownership and profit.

MARIE CLAIRE RESTOUX
1995 WORLD JUDO CHAMPION

Kalaripayat and the Indian Soul

During a trip to the south of India in order to research a film devoted to the history of martial arts (which unfortunately has yet to be made), I discovered Kalaripayat, the southern Indian martial art.

While I was there, I also met P. S. Balachandran, a master of southern-style Kalaripayat, whose family has taught and practiced this art for several generations. With great generosity and patience, he helped me understand its philosophy as well as the connections between Kalaripayat and traditional Indian medicine (ayurveda) and yoga. Master Balachandran also did his best to dispel my ignorance and correct my misapprehensions about India, a land and culture that at first seemed so totally foreign and impenetrable to me. In addition, I met and conversed with other masters as well as practitioners, both young and not so young.

I discovered that, as practiced today, this unusual martial art goes back to the twelfth century, but its history—which is sometimes intertwined with the origins of yoga—certainly goes back several hundred years before our era. At the end of the seventeenth century, Kalaripayat was declared illegal by the British, due no doubt in part to the fact that in 1800, the English Colonel A. Westley fought warriors of the caste known as Nairs who were skilled in the art of Kalaripayat—and he did not emerge victorious! Although it remained banned until India's independence in 1947, its practice and traditions were secretly rescued and preserved by several masters. Today Kalaripayat exists only in the province of Kerala, and is completely unknown in other regions of India or in the world.*

For whatever reason, Kalaripayat has not received the same worldwide attention as karate, judo, kung fu, tai chi, and so on, even though it brings together all forms of combat (internal, external, with weapons) in a remarkable way. Its obscurity is especially astonishing in light of the fact that a number of specialists and researchers consider it to be the elder brother of all Asian martial arts.

Having fallen into almost complete oblivion, Kalaripayat is now experiencing a renaissance through the influence and encouragement of a few masters and because of interest from the international community, which is gradually learning about its many sides. It is very likely that in the years to come it will find its place and become "fashionable" in the Western world. In fact many Western researchers are currently interested in Kalaripayat and a number of books are in preparation that are much more technical than this one.

This book is the result of the investigations of a journalist who has only practiced martial arts a little and whose sole purpose is to have this undeservedly neglected martial art become better known, along with its very specific Indian context, a context burgeoning with spirituality. That is why, before even attempting to approach Kalaripayat, one needs to understand the Indian soul, its mysteries and its contradictions.

---

*There is a combat sport in Portugal known as *jogo do pan,* which resembles Kalaripayat in its sequences. A Portuguese traveler, Luis de Camoens, came to the Malabar coast (of southern Kerala) in the sixteenth century and wrote about Kalaripayat and the Nair warriors who practiced it. He may also have imported their combat techniques into Portugal.

In an immense frothing, a fantastic tumult of sound and color, in the fragile and marvelous silence of the trembling dawn and, upon nightfall, when fish of moonlight dance along the Malabar coast, the life of India exudes, bursts forth, dazzles and overflows—a life that is various, excessive, contradictory and full of drama. India lives and her men and women live along with her, through their joy and their sadness, their good fortune and their bad times, as men and women must do when heart and soul are given outright, without limit, with nothing held back, in laughter and in tears, all being part of the great noise of life. But nothing counts as long as the moment unfolds and the presence of the moment bestows on India the secret of timelessness. And Western youth, tired of growing old and impelled more by intuition than by knowledge, come to drink at the well of this secret. The Ganges never ceases its flow nor do the eyes of men ever cease their caress of its reflections. Yesterday and tomorrow merge (these two words, yesterday and tomorrow, are only one word in Hindi: kal); time is vanquished because it is no longer divided up. And it is perhaps also the perception of the essential that gives India its exceptional and tragic dimension of beauty: the child who comes toward you and holds out his hand to you with a look and a smile of eternity that bares his entire astonished soul. But is there room still for poetry in the modern world, which encroaches here as elsewhere? Can what we call progress be other than a rupture of life in the unfolding of civilizations? Only too late do men realize that they do not live by bread alone.

FRANCIS DORÉ

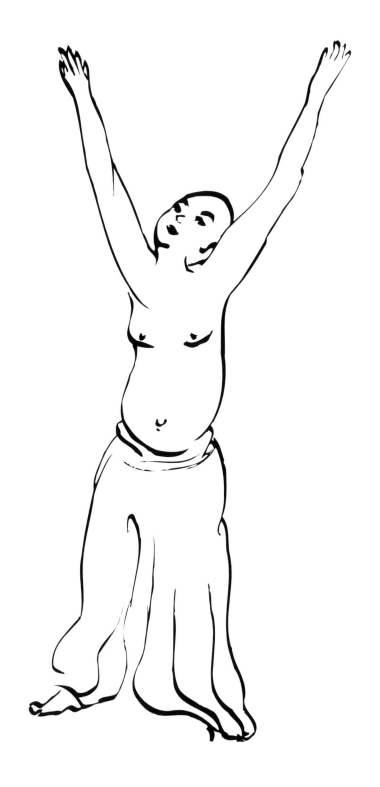

1
The Historical and Philosophical Origins of Kalaripayat

In cases where there is only a choice between cowardice and violence, I recommend violence . . .

I cultivate the quiet courage of dying without killing. But for those who lack this courage, I want them to cultivate the art of killing and being killed, rather than shamefully fleeing danger. Because he who flees commits a mental violence: he flees because he doesn't have the courage to be killed when killing . . .

But I know that non-violence is infinitely superior to violence, and that forgiveness is more manly than punishment.

Forgiveness is the soldier's crowning glory.

GANDHI

KERALA

Forests of coconut palms border the beaches along their
whole length. The extraordinary long and springy
palm leaves seem to play with the gentle breezes, and
softly swaying they lend the air a gentle agitation
extending a coolness up to the ocean waves that are
touched by their shadows.

Images of an earthly paradise with sandy expanses
lined with palms, there you have Kerala.

LEGOUX DE FLAIX, 1788

In the southwest of India lies Kerala, washed on one side by the Indian Ocean and protected on the other by a range of high mountains. With green fields of rice and bouquets of palm trees surrounded by lagoons and golden beaches, Kerala, "land of the palms," is like one big village (see plates 1, 2, and 3 of the color insert). Houses are harmoniously sprinkled in the most unexpected spots; everyone knows each other, and everyone knows all there is to know about their neighbors.

Kerala is India's vast garden. In this wet tropical climate an abundance of all kinds of spices are grown. Shrouded by talipot palms, the gardens around the houses are a jumble of fruit trees, vegetables, and aromatic plants. This region of India is also a center for coconut fiber used in the manufacture of carpets and mats.

This unique region is notable for its geographic isolation since it is cut off from the rest of the country by the Western Ghats, a range of mountains reaching heights of nearly 9,000 feet. However, its lengthy coastline has fostered maritime contacts since ancient times. Its shores were the first areas of Asia known to the West: the Greco-Romans from Alexandria sailed with the monsoon winds that, between June and September, would drive their ships to the

Fig. 1.2. Kerala (shown shaded at the bottom of the map) lies between the mountains and the sea.

"land of spices." Pliny and Ptolemy mention a dozen remarkable spots along this coast, which they called Limyrike, a name borrowed into Greek, in which specialists have discovered the corrupted forms of the Sanskrit words referring to this region as "the holy shore of paradise."

In a surprising land where churches are decorated with Hindu columns, and where Chinese fishing nets sway gracefully along the canals, Kerala shelters a seagoing population. Because of commerce, Kerala was always subjected to new influences throughout the centuries and yet her history was never thrown into chaos by foreign invasions. Today her culture seems to be formed by the same characteristics, combining as it does a spirit of openness, tolerance, and modernity with the traditional conservatism of an incredibly rich heritage.

It is here that Kalaripayat—the most ancient tradition of martial arts in the world—was born. The oldest documents relating to Kalaripayat found in Kerala date from two hundred years before Jesus Christ; they are drawings of fighters carved into palm leaves and then coated with black soot.

AN ORIGIN IN MYTH

We consider it sufficiently proven, that all things arise from their opposite: the weaker from the stronger, the faster from the slower, death from life, and life from death.

SOCRATES

Kalaripayat has its origins in myth: legend glorifies this martial art as having been brought to Kerala by the will of Vishnu and the sage Parasurama in order to protect this newly created land.

It is said that Kerala (also known as Parasuramakshetram) was snatched from the ocean by a courageous Brahmin, one both wise and warlike, whose name was Parasurama ("Rama of the ax"). He was considered to be an incarnation of Vishnu, the deity responsible for the maintenance of the universe. Vishnu protects the moral and cosmic order when it is threatened and periodically descends to earth in a form that suits these purposes.

One legend says that when Vishnu came as Parasurama, he punished the Kshatriyas, the Hindu warrior caste, for their arrogance by exterminating twenty-one generations, which he then atoned for by undergoing a long period of meditation. Another legend says that he was atoning for the decapitation of his mother Renuka.* Ultimately, his long austerities led to his reputation for holiness and earned him the respect of others.

Before becoming a contemplative hermit, Parasurama threw his battle-ax out to sea from Gornaka, on the coast north of Mangalore (at the northern tip of Kerala today). As the ax sank, a strip of land rose up that became Kerala. It is said that after having pulled the country of Kerala from the ocean, Parasurama taught this martial art to his twenty-one disciples so that they could maintain peace.

Palm leaf manuscripts (as shown in figure 1.3) in the possession of certain families who have practiced Kalaripayat for centuries refer to the wise warrior Parasurama as the first guru† of Kalaripayat.

Foremost among Parasurama's pupils was Drona, a master of military science who is one of the heroes of the *Mahabharata,* one of India's two greatest epic poems.§ Drona inherited Parasurama's arms as well as his mission to introduce martial arts to Kerala.

Another great sage in the mythology of Kalaripayat is venerated in the south of Kerala. His name is Agastya Maharshi. A great fighter himself, he taught the art of combat to eighteen disciples who were charged with orally transmitting the art of Kalaripayat.

---

*For yogis, Renuka represents the sperm that they must sublimate before they can achieve total abstinence of desire.

†A guru is a guide who helps his disciples get rid of mental and emotional veils or screens that separate them from reality, allowing them to become aware of their oneness with ultimate reality.

§The *Mahabharata* has had an enormous influence on the thought, customs, festivals, and literature of India and of countries with an Indian civilization.

*Fig. 1.3. Palm leaf manuscripts dating from
the thirteenth century.*

The thoughts of this master are to be found in a thirteenth-century work entitled *Agastya Samhita*. While Agastya is not as prestigious as Parasurama, both of these legendary masters are still venerated by students of Kalaripayat.

NAIR WARRIORS

Man is made for action, just as fire tends to rise and stone tends to fall.

VOLTAIRE

If the geography of Kerala was unique in India, the same was true of its population and the hierarchy of castes. Everywhere else the hierarchy was simple and unique. The Brahmins were the priestly class, responsible for the integration of all acts of civil life with religious rites and duties. They stood at the summit of the pyramid, sharing power and prestige with the warrior Kshatriyas. The Vaishyas, merchants and business people, occupied the center. And right at the base of the pyramid were the Shudras, made up of peasants and tradesmen. The untouchables were kept in the subbasement, beyond the structure of the castes: a simple contact would be enough to soil any member of the higher castes.

In Kerala, only Nambudiri Brahmins* of Malayali lineage occupied the summit. They overshadowed all Brahmins who had come from outside Kerala as well as all the Kshatriyas, except notably those of the warrior class indigenous to Kerala, the Nairs.[†] The pyramid had no middle section, that is, the Vaishyas, since commercial activities in Kerala were carried out by Syrian Christians, Muslims, and Jews. At the base were the Ezhavas who worked in the coconut plantations, and last of all the slaves. Here is an account from the sixteenth century by an anonymous French traveler:

> The caste of Nairs, whose military accomplishments have brought them great privileges, go about half naked armed with a dagger and a sword that never leaves their side. They protect themselves with a round shield and a silk vest. They fight on foot and are skilled in archery and in the use of the spear.
>
> Trained from an early age in military academies, they have

---

*A class of Brahmins originating in Malabar (southern Kerala); being very conservative, they still follow today certain rituals from the India's ancient texts.

[†]The word *Nair* comes from *naga* in Sanskrit (the classical language of India), meaning "serpent." In the courtyards of Nair households, one always finds altars dedicated to serpents.

Fig. 1.4. Warriors in training.

sworn to protect cows and Brahmins. They number several thousand in each of Kerala's kingdoms. They live in large rural properties outside of towns under the authority of mothers and aunts who are guardians of the matriarchal tradition within which they are at liberty to live as they see fit.

Indeed, in the fifteenth century Kerala was made up of small kingdoms of matrilineal* Nair families called Tarawad. The leaders of these families constantly quarreled with one other. In this context Kalaripayat probably attained its greatest flowering; it was an integral part of the social fabric and was widely practiced. It occupied an important place in the education of young Nair, and was a code of conduct and honor for this noble warrior caste of Kerala.

An article in *Karate* magazine envisions a Kalaripayat encounter:

> The two men come face to face, each with a saber in the right hand. Their only clothing is the traditional Indian loincloth. Their black pupils shine with an intense brilliance: they almost seem to be hallucinating. With each movement, light shines from their dark skin and their oil-covered bodies give the scene an unreal quality. Shield in the left hand, they circle very slowly, each one never averting his gaze. The crowd holds its breath. Suddenly, one of the warriors throws himself at his adversary, striking down his saber. The second man parries this first blow and immediately retaliates. An intense, almost wild engagement ensues. Blows rain from all sides with incredible rapidity and with unimaginable violence.
>
> Handling saber and shield without the slightest hesitation,

---

*A type of lineage that recognizes only maternal precedence.

the two opponents are living proof that their dexterity is based on long years of practice. The sound of metal on metal punctuates their martial ballet like a death knell. Suddenly, one of the men slips and loses his balance. His adversary brandishes his saber to deliver a fatal blow. But a guttural cry stops his lunge cold: the crowd parts, standing back respectfully, to allow the passage of a man no longer young. It is the Gurukkal, the master, the man who taught them this deadly art. In the eyes of the two fighters, hate gives way to embarrassment. The master takes them to task in no uncertain terms. How could they, two warrior Nair, the most noble caste of southern India, fight in this way? The Gurukkal is deeply disturbed: did he not teach them that Kalaripayat, Kerala's martial art, is first and foremost a source of life? What shame! Two students from the same kalari, who were trained in the same room, must never attack each other in this way. Embarrassed, the two men fall at their guru's feet, begging his forgiveness. With a gesture, the master invites them to stand and all three move off to the kalari.

Under the tutelage of the village teacher, the Gurukkal, most young Nair boys and even many young girls before the age of puberty were trained in this martial discipline as an important part of the heritage of their caste. Duarte Barbosa, a Portuguese traveler who moved throughout Kerala at the beginning of the sixteenth century, described this indigenous art of war in his travel journal, translated and annotated by Mansel Longworth Dames:

In the Kingdom of Malabar, there is a group of people they call "Nair." They are noblemen whose only duty is to make war. They always carry their weapons with them, swords and lances, bows and arrows. Following a rigorous discipline in life, they

Fig. 1.5. Combat with swords and shields.

never eat more than once a day, do not drink wine, and sleep very little. When they are seven years old, they are sent to the school where they are taught numerous skillful tricks involving agility and dexterity.

They learn dance, whirl on place, how to tumble to the ground, how to make great leaps and other kinds of jumps and they do this twice a day throughout their childhood. Once they have mastered their training, they become so flexible and supple that they can make their bodies do unnatural-looking things. They are taught to play with the weapons with which they have

the greatest affinity: some with bow and arrows, others take up
lances, but they always end by practicing the saber.

The first duty of the heads of Nair families was to train the
region's soldiers and maintain a well-trained army. Duarte Barbosa
brings to life these fighters whose philosophy is close to that of the
nineteenth-century Japanese samurai; he describes with exactness
their way of life and how their cultural and martial heritage was
transmitted from epoch to epoch and dynasty to dynasty.

> The Nair all live with their king and noblemen from whom
> they receive remuneration.
>
> Only those of Nair lineage can become Nair warriors. They
> are entirely devoted to the service of their king or of the high
> nobles; they protect them by carrying weapons day and night.
>
> Some wield bows and arrows, others clubs and lances, but
> most practice with sword and shield which are the most used
> weapons. Training in fencing style is done daily.
>
> The masters who teach them are the Gurukkal who are hon-
> ored and respected by all the students to the extent that they
> are treated like gods. It is both law and custom to bow down
> before them even if the disciple is older than the master. The
> Nair are obliged even if they're old to go and take their fencing
> lesson right up to the time of their death.
>
> Some of the Gurukkal live with the kings and the high
> nobles and do not teach; these would be highly renowned cap-
> tains of war. They promise to die for the king, and in this sci-
> ence of warfare they obtain diplomas as scholars do with us.
> By doing this they receive more generous remuneration than
> other Nair.
>
> Nair of noble lineage must be armed like knights by the

hand of the king. They take an oath to die for the king and if the king is killed they promise to be killed by those who killed the king. If in a battle the master is killed, each Nair will proceed into the midst of the enemy army to die while killing the maximum number of enemy soldiers before dying himself.

For the Nair, combat is a personal affair. Even though there may be a thousand men engaged in a battle, the Nair will avenge his king. He advances alone to meet his opponents, strong in his own science of combat, confident in his own ability to handle his weapons. The Nair are agile and highly skilled, fearless and disdainful of pain.

The rule was that combat must be engaged on an equal footing: if one of the warriors came to be disarmed or if his weapon broke, the battle must continue using bare hands.

There were also warriors called *caveru* (from *cavu,* "death," and *eru,* "speared") who were committed to dying and who belonged to suicide battalions. The existence of suicide battalions is documented in various sources from the ninth century, but they no doubt arose from a much earlier tradition. They were very much a part of the so-called hundred years' war between the Cheras and their neighbors the Cholas, two ancient dynasties who vied for control of south India, in the areas that today are the modern-day states of Kerala and Tamil Nadu, to the east.

For more or less long periods, war and peace alternated during this era and the Nair warriors had no other duties but to train for combat. The king demanded that they keep themselves in top physical shape and, since he maintained a troop that was often numerous and always warlike, engaging in warfare was not only an honor but also served as an outlet for the troublesome moods of the Nair warriors.

Each kingdom had its combat methods. Training took place in the use of the saber and the sword, in handling the spear and the bow, in full-body combat, and in the techniques of meditation. Each warrior in the different kingdoms jealously guarded his own secret techniques, which were in fact matters of life and death for him.

Duarte Barbosa continues:

The Nair live apart from other people in closed communities. When they proceed through the countryside on horseback, they yell at the peasants to get out of their way. If the peasants don't obey they can kill them without fear of retribution.

The Nair enjoy enormous privileges that date back to the beginning of our era. If a peasant has the great misfortune to touch a Nair woman, the Nair would kill the woman immediately as well as the peasant along with the peasant's whole family in order to preserve the purity of the Nair race! When the Nair order work from peasants or buy something from them and in doing so touch the peasants, they must then wash and change their clothes. A Nair will never touch someone from a different caste nor will he eat or drink anywhere but in a Nair household. The Nair are never relieved of their duties by the king and they continue to be paid regardless of their age. If the king does not pay them, they can change kings and their former contract is considered void. . . .

Nair women can have contact with Brahmins but not with people from any of the lower classes on pain of death. When young Nair girls are ten or twelve years old, their mother arranges a marriage ceremony in a strange way. She lets her relatives and friends know that they can come to her home to honor her daughter; then she asks those she has picked out if they agree to marrying her daughter, which generally they do.

The young Nair girl wears on her neck a small gold ornament made up of pearls of gold that are pierced and threaded on a white silk thread. The mother sits beside her daughter who is very well dressed while they and the guests are entertained with music and song. The husband chosen by the mother approaches the daughter and the mother places a gold chain on each of their necks. Then the husband puts the necklace threaded on white silk on his own neck and places his gold chain on the girl's neck. (If she wants, she can choose a different man and put the gold chain on his neck.)

Then the husband moves away and takes his leave without touching her or speaking to her if they are related. If they are not related, he can stay with the woman if he wants, but he doesn't have to.

After this, the mother asks other young men she has chosen if they agree to live with her daughter. If she is very pretty, three or four Nair come together to live with her. The more Nair she has, the more highly is she regarded.

Each man has a designated day with her from noon of one day to noon of the next day. And that is how she spends her life without anyone thinking there is anything the least untoward about the situation.

If one of the men wants to leave her, he does as he wishes. He may leave and take another woman. But if the young Nair girl does not like one of the men, after a certain time she asks him to leave her. He is dismissed and driven away.

The children she bears are the financial responsibility of the mother and her brothers who undertake their education. The children do not know their father and even if one might look like the son of one of the Nair in particular, the child is not recognized nor taken in charge. It is said that these laws were made so that the Nair warrior would not be greedy for profit or possession in any way, and so he would therefore not abandon his service to the king, but would devote himself entirely to the art of war.

The masters wish to perpetuate their ancestors' tradition—even though in our times they no longer live separately from their wives, nor do they have children only to produce more warriors!

THE TEN PRINCIPLES OF KALARIPAYAT

In order not to have fear of losing, we need to have nothing to gain. Losing a victory means that we can bring our mistakes into the light of day and thus be able to modify our actions so that we can move closer to perfection.

Kalaripayat today is a living testimony to the code of conduct and honor of the Nair warriors. Kalaripayat has maintained its purity for hundreds of years by following a definite philosophy that is encoded in ten principles taught by the masters.

1. *Achadakam:* Discipline
2. *Guru Thwam:* Respect for the guru
3. *Krithya Nishta:* Regularity in one's practice
4. *Sakthiyulla Sariram Manasu:* Strength in body and in mind
5. *Kshama:* Patience
6. *Vinayam:* Humility
7. *Manuswathwam:* Humanity
8. *Paramparya Bahumanam:* Respect for tradition

9. *Atmaabhimanam Dheeratha:* Respect for oneself and courage

10. *Shanti:* The search for peace

These principles are the cornerstone of the philosophy of Kalaripayat whose motto is *nithya thozhil abyasam,* or "practice leads the student to perfection."

2
The Practice of Kalaripayat

We must forgive our enemies. If we want to we can kill, but then we might be put in prison and our families would suffer. So we must think of our families and of our enemies' families. We must avoid harming ourselves and we must forgive our enemies. It is easy to strike out and to harm ourselves but that does not authorize us to flee from our responsibilities. . . . What the guru can teach never represents more than one quarter of his pupil's knowledge. One quarter comes from his personal motivation and from his work; another quarter comes by the grace of God, and the final quarter comes to him, in his old age, from experience.

VASUDEVAN GURUKKAL,
MASTER OF KALARIPAYAT

TRAINING IN THE KALARI

*Kalaripayat is a modern system of education. By
mastering energy you attain self-control and overcome
life's difficulties. The student of Kalaripayat is
inculcated with moral responsibility. In this ancient
martial art, effectiveness and physical strength are
supported by respect, attention, and non-violence so
that order is maintained in oneself and in society.*

MASTER PARAMESWARAN
SARASWATHY BALACHANDRAN

Student instruction in Kalaripayat begins at the age of eight with a
ritual initiation conducted by the Gurukkal or master of the *kalari*.
The word *kalari* designates the area with a surface of packed earth
where practice takes place. It is derived from the Sanskrit term *khalutika,* which means "a military training ground." In the palm leaf
manuscripts, which have been handed down from generation to generation, *shastras*, or very strict regulations, prescribe the placement,
orientation, and dimensions of the kalari.

The kalari is always oriented east–west at about four feet below
ground level. Enclosed on all sides except for a small door on the east
side, the dimensions of the kalari are generally 35 feet long by 17.5
feet wide and 17.5 feet high.

If the kalari is not inside a house the roof is made of palm leaves
supported by a bamboo frame.

The construction of the kalari, in the form of an enclosed pit
with very little light, means an airless atmosphere and a constant
temperature favorable for physical training, especially in a tropical
and humid climate such as that of Kerala. Formerly, every village had
its kalari near the ablutions room of the temple.

The kalari is not only a martial training arena; the gymnasium is also a place of assembly and a health care clinic. Most importantly, it is holy ground: a temple for learning the craft and a sanctuary for various gods. The ritual and religious life of Kalaripayat is based on daily worship. Even in modern times, the gods still play an important role in the daily life of masters and students.

Religious Ritual

> *If God's favor is lacking, force is useless.*
>
> PIERRE DE RONSARD

Attending the kalari becomes part of the daily routine for the student, and each day he goes through a series of symbolic rituals before and after the exercises in order to acquire discipline and concentration.

First the student, dressed only in a *kacha* or loincloth, his body covered in oil, prostrates himself before the deities and the Gurukkal. The student always enters the kalari right foot first, touches the earth with his right hand, and then brings his hand to his forehead as a sign of reverence for the holy ground. In the western corner of the kalari is installed an altar: the *puttara*. Several steps lead up to a small platform where incense with the scent of myrrh* burns continually. Here, offerings of flowers are made every day before the glowing light of a small oil lamp. (See plate 4 of the color insert).

The Gurukkal is venerated because he is considered the living representative of the gods and the entire line of gurus in the

---

*A resinous aromatic substance extracted from a shrub, myrrh has always been part of the pharmacopeia of Kalaripayat. It was also recommended for the treatment of wounds by Hippocrates, and was used by the Romans to treat ear and mouth infections and coughs. The Egyptians used it in embalming. According to St. Mark's gospel myrrh as well as wine was offered to Christ before the crucifixion because of its analgesic effects. Today, those effects have been confirmed by pharmacologists.

Fig. 2.2. Religious ritual at the puttara.

Kalaripayat tradition, starting with Parasurama. Since he ensures the continuation of the art, the Gurukkal deserves the same respect as the gods.

The number of gods in the kalari varies from seven to twenty-one and depends on the tradition of each family and of the Gurukkal. The kalari falls under the protection of Bhagavathi, another name for the fearsome goddess Durga, who is usually shown riding on a lion or a tiger and is known for fighting demons. Another of the major gods is Paradevathai, identified as a mixture of Shiva and Shakti.*

The kalari's walls of dark stone impregnated with oil and sweat bear witness to the disciples' efforts as they ritually rub their hands on them. The darkness, the shadows on the walls, the scent of burning myrrh, the beat of the mantra all give the place a spellbinding atmosphere. For a student of Kalaripayat, the ritual and spiritual atmosphere of the kalari plays an important role in the formation of his character and of his attitude toward life.

Although Kalaripayat is above all an educational privilege for young Nair, its teaching developed quickly across religions and castes. Moslems and Christians, having become experts in combat, also worshiped the kalari gods.

Physical Exercises

The relation between the spiritual life and the daily training is embodied in the physical exercises; by carrying out these exercises, the student venerates the protective deities of the kalari with his body and his soul. The importance of physical exercise is highlighted right from the first days of training. (See plates 5 and 6 of the color insert).

---

*Shiva is one of the three major gods of the Brahmanic pantheon, considered as the destroyer; Shakti is a Hindu goddess whose name means "energy." Paradevathai is identified with death and time, but with whom one can curry favor through propitiatory acts.

Kalaripayat requires daily training, rigor, persistence, and encouragement from the master. During the various stages of training, the student learns how to synchronize his physical movements in the sequences he has to learn, developing flexibility in the body and in the mind. Stage by stage, the student overcomes physical difficulties and blockages with the help of the Gurukkal.

It should be noted that a Westerner who practices martial arts generally trains two times a week whereas a practitioner of Kalaripayat trains every day or even twice a day for years in order to reach a good level.

One of the practices that the other Asian martial arts did not borrow from Kalaripayat is the assignment of grades or belts, the *dan,* and so on. In fact, in a kalari everyone is very friendly with one another and the master knows all his students. So it isn't necessary to identify a student's level by assigning him a grade.

In Kalaripayat there are no combat competitions—therefore no victor and no victory—but only demonstrations of different sequences between two adversaries. In the past if a battle was fought, it could end only with the death of one of the two combatants. Unlike other martial arts practiced in the world, Kalaripayat demonstrations take place with real weapons and not wooden or imitation ones, which means that the student can get seriously hurt if the precision of his blocking of an attack is a little off. Nowadays, the ultimate goal is self-knowledge, so the only adversary to be overcome is oneself.

COMBAT SYSTEM

The fundamental principle of Kalaripayat is somewhat close to aikido: the adversary must never manage to reach you. Therefore the feint (dodge or sidestep) is of prime importance in this art. The second important point is that the force of the mind is decisive in this combat because everything depends on using intention and not physical force.

Kalaripayat makes very little use of strikes with the fist. It does, however, use jumps and blows with the feet, similar to the *mae geri* practiced in karate, but delivered from high up. There is also a lateral blow with the foot and a circular one as well. Kalaripayat has a unique and special form of blocking: an attack with the fist at the level of the adversary's face is rebuffed with a foot strike from high up. (See plate 7 of the color insert.)

The training is mainly divided into three parts called *meithari, kolthari,* and *ankathari.* During meithari, which is a series of exercises to prepare the body, the student learns various stretching movements for the legs, the basic positions for the body, jumps, and flexibility exercises, all of which make up the first part of the system. In the advanced stages of meithari, the guru teaches the student several exercises to control the body. They help him sense his balance and the continuous flow of energy that circulates through his organism.

As the student is introduced to specific, graded exercises and then sequences of them, his progress is watched closely by the Gurukkal, who assesses his level in each technique. Only when he is satisfied does he introduce the student to the practices using weapons in the kolthari and ankathari stages.

The Suvadus: Bare-Hand Techniques

The thick jungle that entirely covers Kerala from the mountains to the sea—along with the many wild animals living in it—are part of Kalaripayat's beginnings. The observation of wild animals gave birth to *asata vadivu,* the eight techniques of bare-hand attack and defense, which are modeled on the postures of eight wild animals. When an animal fights, it uses its whole body; it's the same in Kalaripayat.

Fig. 2.3. Bare-hands combat.

The *maippayat,* or sequences of these eight techniques, are similar to the *tao* or basic movements of kung fu, which are also based on observing animals. These prescribed exercises are combinations of movements of the body (*meitolil*), which include stances (*vativu*), steps (*cuvat*), and strikes with the feet (*kaletupp*). They include a variety of jumps and turns, as well as movements with synchronized arms and hands, which are executed more and more quickly.

These eight sequences are not static forms but are drawn from the essential internal or external nature of the animal.

- The horse concentrates all his energy in his chest, and rears up in order to jump. This same posture is found in the *asvavadivu* pose.
- When the peacock has to attack his enemies, he makes a fan with his plumage, he stretches up his neck, dances, and comes to rest on one foot. Then he puts his whole weight on the other foot and attacks by jumping and flying. The attack copied from this animal is called *mayuravadivu.*
- A serpent attacks his enemies by drawing himself up while his tail remains motionless on the ground. From this position he can turn in any direction to bite. This ability to turn in any direction for attack or defense while standing on one leg is called *sarpavadivu.*
- When the rooster attacks, he uses all parts of his body—his wings, his neck, his feet, and his claws. He raises one leg, ruffles his feathers, moves his neck, and looks at his enemy with a fixed stare. Then he attacks. This pose is called *kukkuvadivu.*
- When a tiger jumps, he pulls his whole body back to accumulate a maximum amount of energy, then pushes violently on his paws and stretches out his body. This position is called *kutichu chadi.*

The masters speak of the importance of the eight stances in their students' progress; they feel that only those who learn these stances perfectly can claim to know the law of hitting (*mura*) and progress to fight with bare hands or weapons, to practice massage, or to acquire a knowledge of pressure points.

Moving Like Water

The bare-hand techniques are practiced in sequences similar to the *ragas** of Indian music, which repeat the same musical pattern endlessly. Water symbolizes the fluidity of Kalaripayat gestures and movements. Moving between positions must be done just like water that always assumes the shape of its container to perfection.

The same movements and the various on-guard stances are repeated facing east, facing west, facing north, and facing south, so one learns to be ready for anything. Master Balachandran maintains: "It is more difficult and therefore more dangerous to fight with bare hands than to fight with weapons. When you fight with weapons, you must concentrate on the opponent's weapon; when you fight with the hands, you must concentrate on the opponent's entire body. If you are hit, you have to concentrate on another part of the body and ignore the part that has just been hit."

The name of the base posture in Kalaripayat is *nilachuvadu*. It allows you to respond to an attack with an immediate block and to reengage using a strike with the fist (like the *uraken* used in karate) or a foot strike with the body weight on the rear foot. The first rule of the on-guard stance is always to stay three steps away so that your opponent cannot hit you. The position is lower than that used in other martial arts. (See plates 8 and 9 of the color insert.) It is done in this way:

- Turned three-quarters toward the adversary, feet very flat on the ground, knees open.
- The back is rounded and the trunk is inclined slightly forward.

---

*A blending of modes and rhythms intended to awaken a variety of sensations and emotions in the listener.

- The shoulders are naturally lowered, the arms lightly flexed and crossed in front of the lower part of the body.
- The look is fixed on the opponent.

All moves take place from this position; the foot that moves is on the side facing the direction one wants to go.

There are many positions, and they each they depend on the opponent—his size, his weight, how aggressive he is, how he carries himself, his jumping around, and so on. Some of these positions are:

- *Kuthi nilpu*: when the opponent delivers strikes with the feet.
- *Vatta chuvadu*: to reduce the opponent's angle of attack and then feint.
- *Nedum cuvadu*: when combat is under way using weapons.

One has to be able to move from one position to another quickly. To achieve this and do it with ease takes hours of practice. (See plates 10 and 11 of the color insert.)

Techniques of Falling

Falls (*vizhu*) are practiced to avoid contact with the opponent. They are part of every training session and are repeated until they become completely automatic.

- Tackling the ground: this energetic movement consists of falling straight down on the spot. The legs are thrown up high and toward the rear while the body is allowed to fall horizontally, landing on the hands and cushioned by flexed arms. The practitioner then springs right back up using both the arms and the legs.

- Falling forward (*purake vizhuka*): this is a fall forward, landing on open hands and cushioned by flexed arms. The head remains in line looking forward. One gets up by pushing vigorously with the arms and returning to a very low on-guard position.
- Falling backward (*munpe vizhuka*): this is done by bending the legs completely, rounding the back, chin down to the chest. The practitioner does a roll on the back but avoids taking the whole weight of the body on the spine. One leg is kept bent and the other is extended ready to fend off the opponent.

It is essential to keep the gaze firmly fixed on the opponent, and to get up by swaying the body forward while reestablishing support through the knee of the bent leg and the hand on the same side, as the body rotates. One also needs to move up into a position that allows feinting, which means in the direction away from the opponent. For example, this would be done by rotating the body to the right and using the support of the right knee and the right hand, with the right arm extended as an extension of the shoulders, and extending the left arm and leg to the right and to the rear, and then rising using all four limbs.

WEAPONS

One of the riches of Kalaripayat is its use of weapons, some of which exist in no other discipline. This is true of the wooden club-like *ottakkol* and the flexible metal *urimi*. In former times, more than ten weapons were used in Kalaripayat; today only four or five are commonly used. The complex weapon techniques discussed here are designed to gain complete control over the weapon by making it an extension of the body. To reach this level one needs to spend several continuous years of practice under a Gurukkal's supervision.

Second Stage (Kolthari) Weapons

Under a sword raised high, hell makes you tremble, but move forward and you will find the land of happiness.

The second phase of training, kolthari, involves training with wooden weapons such as the *kettukari,* a simple bamboo pole, thin and very long (about six feet). Blows to various parts of the body are exchanged and parried with this weapon; either end is used very skillfully. (See plates 12 and 13 of the color insert.) Training with the kettukari makes handling the spear easier. Another type of weapon is the viada (a heavy, two-handed club). (See plate 14 of the color insert.)

The *cheruvati* is a solid, heavy stick, fairly short, made of a kind of bamboo. Blows are exchanged and parried in quick succession, sometimes at the rate of 200 a minute. The cheruvati is used both for attack and defense.

The *ottakkol,* the third weapon taught to the student, plays a pivotal role in his progress. The ottakkol is a special weapon that serves as a working tool to coordinate complex movements of the body as well as step patterns. It is wooden with a specially curved shape and has a handle at one end and a small club at the other.

More than a weapon, the ottakkol is a master's tool reserved for the highest level of Kalaripayat; various strikes, thrusts, and holds of a high technical level are used. The thrusts are aimed at hitting the body's pressure points. Whereas all the other weapons have twelve training sequences, the ottakkol has eighteen.

Handling this weapon requires suppleness, endurance, liveliness, and great dexterity. Whoever masters this technique is definitely a master of unarmed combat. Slithering like a snake or leaping like a leopard, he can defend himself, and disarm, maim, or even kill his opponent with his bare hands. This weapon helps in the transition to performing Kalaripayat's advanced techniques accurately.

The *urimi*, an amazing weapon, is a long and flexible sword, worn around the body like a belt. One needs to move very fast when handling the urimi, and its effectiveness is fearsome when there are many assailants. In Kerala folklore, there are many legends about Kalaripayat: it is said that with his urimi a fighter is capable of cutting through a leaf pasted on the stomach of a young boy without wounding him. The techniques of this flexible, double-bladed sword were employed in mass confrontations of Nair warriors. The warriors of olden times wound the urimi around their belts and were able to draw it in one quick movement and neatly slice off their opponent's head.

Third Stage (Ankathari) Weapons

The third and last phase is ankathari, or combat exercises with weapons made from unbending metal.

The training begins with the *kattaram,* a metallic weapon that is a kind of dagger used in combat duels fought at close range. Several holds and numerous elements of bare-hands combat technique are taught for efficient dagger practice. The dagger is used both for attack and defense. Great skill, alacrity, and liveliness in movement are necessary for its use. Most often the fighting involves close body contact, and the slightest lapse of attention can lead to serious injury. (See plates 15 and 16 of the color insert.)

The sword and shield (shown in figure 2.4) were the arms used by the medieval soldiers of Kerala and are the prime combat arms

Fig. 2.4. Sword and shield combat.

in the Kalaripayat system. Training in the sword and shield draws on the complete range of movements learned in the preliminary physical training exercises. When a skilled practitioner is able to demonstrate mastery in their use, he can claim to have attained a very high level in the art of Kalaripayat. (See plates 17, 18, and 19 of the color insert.)

The art of the sword and shield involves complex engagements that seem both artistic and stylized, from the initial salutation between contestants to the dynamic sessions of *puliyankam,* or "leopard combat."

Fig. 2.5. Sword and shield combat.

References to many of Kalaripayat's sword and shield techniques are found in the fourth-century texts of the *Agni Purana** and the *Natya Shastra.*† One legend has it that once a sword is drawn from its case, it must not be put back without being stained in blood.

The rich and complex repertoire of Kalaripayat armament also includes the techniques of great precision required when fighting with the spear as well as the classic sessions of combat with the mace, the weapon of the epic heroes.

There is also the *marapititcha kuntham,* a duel between a man with a sword and a man armed with a spear. For each of the opponents, a precise skill is demanded that is specific to his weapon.

Kathiyum thalayum or *uruloy,* a spectacular technique of cloth against knife, is practiced during demonstrations. It involves a battle between two partners, one with a dagger and the other equipped only with the towel that the Keralites wear on their shoulders for wiping away sweat.

Before each armed combat, the fighters salute each other: this is the *mukhakettu,* which celebrates the principle of loyal combat.

Weapons That Are Thrown

> *You must always aim farther than the target.*

The medieval soldiers of Kerala fought also with the *cakra,* a thrown weapon, which is very little used in our day except in a few of the kalari in the east side of Kerala. Thrown weapons in traditional India were classified into four kinds: *yantramukta* (thrown by machines),

---

*A traditional Sanskrit text dealing with various subjects such as the creation of the world, legends, and mythologies, composed in an encyclopedic form of twelve thousand stanzas.

†A treatise on dance, in Sanskrit, which contains all knowledge relating to dance, music, and the art of theater.

Fig. 2.6. Fighting with spears.

panimukta (thrown by hand), *muktasandharita* (thrown and retrieved), *mantramukta* (thrown with the help of curses or imprecations).

The cakra is mentioned in the *Mahabharata* and in the *Agni Purana* among twenty-eight warfare devices. It is classified in the panimukta group, and is defined as being like a razor. It is fashioned in the shape of an iron ring whose outside edge is beveled to a very sharp cutting blade. In technical terms it would be called an orbicular knife, or more simply a kind of disc. It is thrown by the warrior, who makes it spin in order to split, slice, or cut.

We learn of its terrifying effects from certain epic texts: Kali (the goddess representing the destructive power of time), Vishnu, and other divine personages use it in combat to sever their enemies' heads, heads that because of the sudden, clean cut, "remain for a moment on their victims' shoulders before falling off."

In the sixteenth century, Duarte Barbosa records in his notebooks that these "steel wheels," which he calls *characani,* are "two fingers wide, sharpened on the outside edge like knives and with no cutting surface inside; their surface is about the dimension of a small plate." He adds, "They each carry seven or eight strung together on the left arm. Taking one and placing it on the finger of the right hand, they spin it several times and then they hurl it at their enemies. If it hits the arm, leg, or neck of any one of them, it cuts the appendage right off."

Held in the hand, in spite of its sharp edge, a cakra can even be thrown like a flat stone and made to skip across water. There is a clear similarity with certain *shaken,* the thrown weapons used by *ninja** warriors.

Bow and Arrow

> *At one extremity of his bow, the archer pierces the sky,*
> *at the other he enters the earth; stretched between the*
> *two, the bowstring launches the arrow to the heart of*
> *the target—a target visible and invisible.*

There is no art in ancient India that is more highly considered than archery. It is the symbol of gods and heroes and arouses an epic vigor that evokes supreme victory. The archer's knowledge is

---

*In Japan a class of men specially trained for espionage and assassination created at the end of the Heian period (794–1185). Legend has seized upon the image of the *ninja* and extraordinary powers were attributed to them, such as being able to make themselves invisible or walking on the ceiling.

associated with heroism and the tales are full of the miracles of legendary archers. Simply put, the practice of archery can be compared to a holy practice.

As Duarte Barbosa describes the practice of Kalaripayat, we learn that each Nair warrior practiced archery after, and only after, having mastered his own body. During the battle of 1758 with the Dutch at Kulachal (southern tip of India), the Nair used bows, but the bow was abandoned when firearms appeared.

The student who practices archery must, before all else, learn to adopt the various positions that will then allow him to hit the most difficult targets. He also must know the various categories of bows and of arrows and learn to judge distances. Then he has to work at and practice meditation techniques that are specific to archery.

Archery Stances

The stances that the student must learn are numerous. The *Agni Purana* enumerates ten in the chapter on *Dhanur Veda,* the science of archery:

1. *Samapada:* standing, with ankles, calves, and thighs tightly together; the palms of the hands and the thumbs touching.
2. *Vaishakha:* standing on tiptoe, thighs touching; the feet apart by 3 *vitasti* (or 12 *angula,* or about 8 inches).
3. *Mandala:* the thighs rounded like the wings of a swan; the feet 5 *vitasti* apart.
4. *Alidha:* the right leg bent, the left held diagonally; the knees 5 *vitasti* apart.
5. *Pratyalidha:* the left leg bent; the right held diagonally.
6. *Sthanam:* the legs apart and bent, the knees 5 *angula* apart with the whole of the position not exceeding a width of 12 *angula.*

7. *Jata:* heels close together, left leg straightened, the right bent
   slightly.
8. *Vikata:* the right leg vertical and straight as a reed, the left
   stretched at a slightly diagonal angle, with a space of 2 cubits
   (3 feet) being maintained between the position of the feet.
9. *Samputa:* lying down, the legs raised, the knees bent and
   crossed.
10. *Svastika:* standing, the legs completely straight and stiff, the
    feet 16 *angula* apart, toes pointing out.

Shooting an Arrow

Adopting one of these positions, the student grasps the bow in his
left hand and the arrow in his right hand, then he flexes the bow
using a string that has been dyed red. The *Agni Purana* specifies
that the string must be neither too long nor too short. The archer
raises his bow and places the feathered end of the arrow on the
string so that there's a distance of 12 *angula* between the bow and
the string.

Keeping the bow at the level of his navel and tossing his quiver
round to his lower back, he raises the bow with his left hand until it
is on a level with the sockets of his eyes and the hollow passages of
his ears. The *Agni Purana* also mentions that he must not pull the
string so forcefully back that the head of the arrow is inside the curve
of the bow, nor should he pull it so weakly that the arrow does not
go far enough outside of the bow. To achieve this, the *Agni Purana*
carefully defines the extension that must be maintained between the
string and the bow, depending on what kind of arrow is used. For a
first-class arrow, a space of 3 angula must be maintained between the
chin and the tip of the shoulder; for a second-class arrow this distance would be 2 angula, and only one for a third-class arrow.

The *Agni Purana* goes on to explain how the archer, having

trained his attention on his chosen target—his one and only point—and while holding his head firm and his neck very still, his chest expanded and his shoulders down, the whole upper body forming a triangle, he then lets his arrow fly.

The difficulties in archery are not only about hitting the target, but have to do also with the position of the archer in relation to his target. The *Agni Purana* classifies them into three categories:

1. Targets that require a particularly firm hand: required with objects that have dull surfaces or sharp edges, or those that fall on the archer's line of sight.
2. Targets that are difficult to reach: objects that are situated above or below the line of sight.
3. Targets that are exceptionally difficult: ones placed between the highest point and the archer's head or directly above him.

The *Agni Purana* tells us that when the student has been able to overcome all these difficulties, he then undergoes an examination with his teacher and if he is deemed worthy, he will be allowed to practice his art on horseback.

Legendary Archery

If the archer's strength becomes peerless, so does his skill. Following numerous exercises and long inner work, the archer may claim that he can hit a target without being able to see it. The *Mahabharata* gives the example of an archer who fired seven arrows into the snout of a dog that he could not see but that he heard barking. Real exploits of the practitioners of this art are mixed with legend.

Arrows, with their magic power, are of precious assistance to the archer. Numerous incantations allow the arrow to proceed toward its target and then come back again: "after having run through seven trees, the arrow crossed the mountain plain and penetrated the earth to its seventh level; then it returned and placed itself in the quiver." We find in certain texts that the Nair warriors sometimes used poisoned arrows.

Archery and Meditation

The vast horizon of the two eyes serves only to distract the sight, but if you achieve a unified vision, your sighting will be exact and your aim will be set.

The *Mahabharata* tells a story of a test given to his royal students by Drona, the famous Brahmin archery teacher. This test demonstrates how the practice of meditation and spiritual concentration is an element that can determine victory during a battle. For this test, Drona called before him each prince to see if he would be able to fire an arrow into the lock of a birdcage that was placed in a tree. Every prince failed this test except Prince Arjuna. They failed for the simple reason that none of them, except Arjuna, had developed and worked on what Drona called *ekagrata,* that is, a "sole point of concentration": a sublime concentration in which the lock and the shot merge, where the release and the impact are one single reality.

Another time Drona asked his students how they saw the target, which was an eagle perched on a treetop. The first two saw Drona, the tree, and the eagle. But Arjuna said, "I see only the bird. I see his head but not his body." Drona gave him the order to shoot and the bird's head, severed by the arrow, fell to the ground. This is an example of contemplative vision: "The body is the bow, the arrow is Om, the mind is the tip of the arrow, and the target is darkness." More of these kinds of relationships could be mentioned, since the symbolism of archery and the training it demands are very connected to ascetic practices.

In Kerala, there is a saying of popular wisdom that sums up the psychophysical and respiratory state of the ideal martial arts practitioner. This ideal state takes place when: "the whole body becomes an eye" (*meyya kannakuka*). If someone intuitively embodies this popular expression in his practice of the martial art, he will develop not only the "sole point of concentration" but also the ability to sense intuitively his entire environment.

It is clear that the development of such advanced mental and physical sensitivity is not achieved except through continuous practice and not simply through exercises in which you wound, mutilate, or kill, but rather through exercises leading to restraint, control, and humility. Perhaps here we have in fact the principal characteristics of the artful martial practitioner.

Cultivating the "sole point of concentration" means to cultivate the body and mind so that together they are one eye; it means to cultivate your deep nature or essentially to cultivate your "I." Such an approach leads to an inner force and therefore to a state of inner peace described accurately in the *Agni Purana*: "He who has steadied his eye's vision—both mental and physical—can vanquish even Yama, the god of death; vanquishing Yama means first of all vanquishing oneself."

NORTHERN STYLE AND SOUTHERN STYLE

Suppleness can control hardness; weakness can control force.

Kalaripayat can be divided into two general styles, which are likely related to how the country is shaped and where various groupings of the population live.

The northern style developed among people who inhabit the interior of the country; they live in the countryside and work the land. In the north Kalaripayat is not often practiced with weapons; essentially they fight with the body. This style uses jumps and blows with the feet from very high up; long strides; a very compact on-guard stance; and strikes and blocks with the arm and hand almost outstretched. In the sequences, an important place is given to the work of the feet.

The southern style, practiced by the seaside populations, makes much greater use of weapons. According to the masters, this difference is because of the Dutch presence in the seventeenth century and the armed resistance to it. This style involves circular movements; strikes and blocks done with the open hand and the arm flexed; a higher on-guard stance. The use of powerful movements of the arms and torso is particularly notable.

3
The Psychology of Combat

Finally, the combat begets the element of danger, in
which all the activities of War live and move, like
the bird in the air or the fish in the water. But the
influences of danger all pass into the feelings, either
directly—that is instinctively—or through the medium
of the understanding. The effect in the first case
would be a desire to escape from the danger, and, if
that cannot be done, fright and anxiety. If this effect
does not take place, then it is courage, which is a
counterpoise to that instinct. Courage is, however, by
no means an act of the understanding, but likewise
a feeling, like fear; the latter looks to the physical
preservation, courage to the moral preservation.
Courage, then, is a nobler instinct. But because it
is so, it will not allow itself to be used as a lifeless
instrument, which produces its effects exactly according
to prescribed measure. Courage is therefore no mere
counterpoise to danger in order to neutralize the latter
in its effects, but a peculiar power in itself.
CARL VON CLAUSEWITZ, *ON WAR*, 1827

FEAR (*BHAYAM*)

Kill ambition,
kill the desire for life,
kill the desire for well being,
kill the feeling of separation,
kill the desire for sensing,
kill the desire for more,
and be; in this way fear will disappear.

BUDDHA

Fear is a more or less instinctive natural reaction engendered by a real or imaginary cause. There is no way to eliminate it since it is a mechanism of warning and protection vital to the organism. The problem is that this alarm can often sound inappropriately and draw heavily on the individual's energetic reserves. Its symptoms are well known to everyone: legs that won't run, breath short and halting, profuse sweating, stomach in a knot.

The Kalaripayat fighter needs fear but he must control it and not let it dominate. To make his fear disappear he needs to attack; he must never think of himself. He has to make the fear work in the spiritual sphere, using it to generate energy.

Like all emotions, fear depends on the autonomic nervous system that regulates our emotional and biological life. To control emotions such as fear and anguish, the Nair had recourse to a series of *mudra*[*]-like gestures—essentially finger movements—combined with certain vibrations emitted by the vocal cords as a *mantra*.[†]

---

[*]Mystical gestures of the hands symbolizing the powers and mental attitudes of Hindu and Buddhist deities and spiritual masters.
[†]A sacred Hindu or Buddhist formulation that distills into a material form the deity that it is intended to evoke. Mantras arose for the most part from the sacred syllable "OM."

An example of a mudra can be seen in the *abhaya mudra.* *Abhaya,* a Sanskrit term generally applied to deities, means "without fear." In this mudra—which symbolizes the absence of fear or protection—the right palm is held at the level of the shoulder, facing out with the fingers pointing up. It can be combined with other mudras in the other hand.

The Nair traditionally combined the use of mudras and mantras with mental concentration on a particular nerve plexus or psychic center. This area is located around the seventh thoracic vertebra. The capacity to do this was developed by a meditative practice. "Seated in meditation position, hold the in-breath and during this time concentrate on this vertebra with the intent of sending it warmth. Breathe out slowly while keeping your awareness focused on this region. In order to obtain results, this method must be practiced regularly for many years."

LOOKING AHEAD AND ANTICIPATING IN COMBAT

If you are not as good as your opponent, make peace. If you have gathered forces to oppose him, make war. If you have concluded, "Neither can my opponent destroy me, nor can I destroy him," then wait.

KAUTLIYA, 400 BCE

As we have seen, the expression "the body becomes an eye" sums up the way in which the Kalaripayat masters see their art. This ideal state can be interpreted in light of the yogic concept of a "unity of mind and body." In this unity, you are able to respond intuitively to the sensory environment and to be fluid in relation to your environment.

Like Brahma* with his thousand eyes, the accomplished practitioner can see all, sense danger intuitively, and respond immediately. In ancient times, in a world where power was traditionally unstable and violent, this kind of response was essential in order to respond with a simple glance or gesture, either to a simple poke in the stomach or to the real possibility of an attack.

A Kalaripayat master makes it clear to his student that he needs to know when his opponent is afraid. A person is afraid if he is always bobbing around, or if his face is pale. Also, his increased heartbeat will show in panting and trembling, there will be weakness in his moves, and his pupils will be dilated. When the opponent is afraid he will pull back a little and will be more inclined to use his feet in attacking. His movements will be hesitant. Fear means that he will keep his distance at first, then attack in an uncontrolled way. A clenched fist is a sign of anger and an intention to respond quickly.

When a Nair warrior was on a mission, his solar plexus would function like radar and he could instinctively sense any danger that threatened his life. In developing this particular area of the body, he would master his fear and the sensation of danger would be transmitted to him and interpreted as a precise image. This meant that the fighter would be capable of knowing exactly where his enemies were located and how many men were waiting in ambush.

USE OF THE EYES IN COMBAT

*Once you have practiced Kalaripayat for a long time,
you will be able to anticipate the opponent's attack*

---

*The god of the Hindu trinity responsible for creation; he is the lord of heaven and master of the horizon.

*simply by watching his eyes: right before his attack, his
eyes will move imperceptibly in the direction that the
attack will come from. You must seize that moment,
but it is only with a lot of practice that you will succeed.*

Someone proficient in Kalaripayat does not back off and will keep looking his opponent in the eye in order to anticipate his next move. He has to know how to seize the opportunity the moment his adversary is most vulnerable. He will watch his opponent's eyes in order to know his intentions, while maintaining a wide-ranging view in order to follow his opponent's gestures and movements. (See plate 20 of the color insert.)

He needs to decode the position of his opponent's eyes: if anger is controlled and there is self-assurance, the eyes close slightly, whereas with fear, they are dilated. He also needs to be able to catch the palpebral reflex (an imperceptible movement of the eyelids) that gives advance warning of his next move.

In combat it is necessary to visualize an opponent's weapons without looking at them. It is also very important not to stand still, but always to keep moving, since an opponent will have great difficulty hitting a target that never stays still.

Kalaripayat teaches that—when faced with several opponents—the practitioner's look must be fixed on the one closest while he keeps all the others in his field of vision. They eyes must remain focused on one opponent at a time and on the upper part of his body, while an overview of the whole scene is also maintained. If he wants to win, he must attack first, choosing the closest, most aggressive opponent. He must keep the upper hand by choosing an angle that makes it hard for the others to intervene. This is done by getting the chosen adversary into a position in front of the others so he forms an obstacle or a screen.

SHOUTING
WITH THE ATTACK

When a master goes by, the dogs don't bark.

Shouting is certainly one of the first reactions to danger whether it's to call for help or to warn friends. The fact that a cry may cause wavering in an enemy's aggressive intentions or even stop an attack is perhaps the basis of the active use of the human voice as a strategic element in combat arts. All fighting societies in the past have certainly used it quite freely.

The Greek and Roman legions were well acquainted with the paralyzing effect of a clamor rising suddenly from the depth of a silent forest. They engaged in ferocious howls or took full advantage of the din of their various arms.

Paradoxically, silence is Kalaripayat's cry. There is no *kiai* used to free up energy as in karate or other martial arts. The silent cry comes from the depths of the practitioner's being. It projects a subtle energy and the breath liberates this energy. This silence is unified with the vital force and is an emanation of it. Silence is an immense cry that emits a vibration that unsettles the adversary. Tradition says that whoever knows how to use this silent cry will be a conqueror and a destroyer.

Silence is of incomparable sophistication in the art of Kalaripayat since it requires no physical contact between adversaries. The combat techniques or strategies are reduced to a maximum expansion of pure, immaterial energy. It is invisible to the naked eye, inaudible by the ear, and participates in overcoming the weaker of the two adversaries. Years of training are required to achieve perfection in this silence, which then has the power to avert an adversary's assault.

Master Balachandran remarks with a smile: "When there is combat in our art, the cry comes from the one who is hit."

4

Kalaripayat and Traditional Indian Medicine

A weak body weakens the mind.

J. J. ROUSSEAU

No person is truly free if he is a slave of the body.

SENECA

It is said that in the field of medicine, there was a book, now lost, that was composed by the god Brahma. It was in the form of a poem of one hundred thousand verses, but he communicated it to humans only in the form of a summary. This book was called the *Ayur Veda*, and the title could be translated as "those who know life." This book is said to have given birth to traditional Indian medicine, also known as *ayurveda*, the science (*veda*) of long life (*ayus*).

At the time of the invasion of the Aryans, about 800 BCE, the

57

far more ancient medical principles were set down in doctrines that are found in the four Vedas (generic name given to the most ancient Indian texts). At that time, illness and healing were above all considered to be the work of the gods. Healing was to be obtained through prayer and magical formulas and through the use of medicinal plants. Homeopathic concepts and the techniques of operations were already very advanced.

The era beginning around 800 BCE, known as the Brahmanic era, is considered the golden age of Hindu medicine. Numerous manuscripts were produced containing doctrines that influenced the whole era. This period is particularly noted for its humanitarian tendencies, for the foundation of hospitals, for its training systems for doctors, and so on.

Later, beginning in the year 1000, Hindu medical doctrines began to be combined with and greatly influenced by Arabic medicine.

In India, medicine and the science of pharmacology are not independent sciences nor are they based solely on empiricism. Instead they are intimately connected with the general civilization of which they are an integral part, as well as being closely related to its metaphysical and philosophical concepts. That is why a medical treatment will simultaneously take into account astrological and time of day considerations, invocations to divine powers, and physical medications. A human being is considered to be a whole in which body, mind, and spirit are inseparable.

THE HEALING ROLE OF
THE GURUKKAL

Kalaripayat's exercises and body mastery play a large role in the ayurvedic medicine that is practiced in Kerala. This combination of

Kalaripayat, martial arts, and medicine is unique in the world. As a result, the Gurukkal plays the double role of a master in martial arts and a healer or doctor. (See plate 21 of the color insert.) It takes long years of experience as a student, significant training, his master's confidence, and a good attitude to transform a student into a Gurukkal who will direct a kalari.

Each Gurukkal has received special teaching relating to the practice of medicine in the Kalaripayat system, one that is based on ayurveda and enhanced by contributions from former Kalaripayat masters. This system of treatment, called *kalarichikitsa,* specializes in orthopedic injuries and nervous disorders. During exercises in the kalari, it is not unusual for someone to be wounded by the various weapons or to dislocate a joint following a violent shock. The manual form of therapy particular to Kalaripayat grew out of the need to treat wounds, fractures, and dislocations on the spot in the training centers in Kerala.

Still very much alive today, traditional Indian medicine is a very ancient knowledge that is both empirical and rational. A good doctor must pay particular attention to external signs that reflect the internal state of the individual. To do this, he must look at the state of the hair, the skin, the eyes, the tongue, the nails, the breath, saliva, and speech.

The Gurukkal's teaching also includes specialization in the preparation of herbs. Each school has its own recipes and methods, but the herbs that make up formulas are often the same. It is noteworthy that in Kerala the pharmacopeia of ayurvedic medicine has included for hundreds of years substances that our modern pharmacopeia has included only in the past fifty years, such as ephedrine, an organic substance extracted from branches of a shrub of the genus *ephedra*. It is used to relieve congestion in the nostrils, as well as to dilate the pupils and bronchial passages (in treating asthma). As early as the fifteenth century, Indian doctors also used mercury to fight syphilis. They would insert into the nostrils of the patient little rolls of paper that contained red mercuric sulfate, which they would then set on fire.

The most eminent doctors and masters have classified plants according to their nature (fruit trees without flowers, fruit trees with flowers, herbs that have a stalk, climbing plants, etc.). They have observed them through their stages of growth and then have further classified herbs according to their recognized medicinal properties. According to them, all plants are endowed with procreative male and female energy, as well as dynamic and static properties that can be used to reestablish balance in the organism.

In this way a list of 436 plants came to belong to the body of ayurvedic medical knowledge. They were then used to diminish or relieve pain, but more importantly to reestablish the organic balance that has been compromised by a lack or excess of internal or external bodily secretions. Ayurveda refers to three bodily humors—wind, phlegm, and fire—that need to be in balance for good health. Their role is explained in a text by Sushruta, a famous Indian doctor of the first century, to whom the composition of numerous ayurvedic medical treatises is attributed.

The *Gurukkal* uses this concept to care for his patients. According to popular belief, when Kalaripayat is practiced daily, it balances the three bodily humors. The practice of massage is also intended to maintain balance among the three humors. The following is a notable passage from Sushruta:

The act of making efforts with the body is called exercise; after exercise one ought to shampoo the body all over until an agreeable and comfortable sensation is obtained.

Physical exercise produces a lively energy in the body, a building up of the body while providing harmonious proportions in the arms and legs. No enemy will attack a man who practices exercise since the attacker will be afraid of that person's strength. Senility does not overtake the practitioner quickly and his muscles stay firm. For someone who practices exercise and who is massaged with the feet of a masseur, illnesses will run from him like little beasties who catch sight of a lion. Physical exercise bestows a good appearance even on those who are no longer young or who are not handsome. When exercise is practiced well, even the most difficult food can be digested without affecting or disturbing the bodily humors, including food that has turned bitter or is mediocre. Physical exercise can help a strong man who has eaten greasy food. The training, which is especially beneficial in the winter and spring, should be done every day regardless of the season and up to about half way to the limit of the strength of the person who is training. Doing more than that could kill him. When the froth that is usually in the heart of the person practicing physical exercise rises up into his mouth that is the sign that he has used half his strength.

In doing physical exercise one needs to take into consideration age, strength, body, location, time of day, and food. Only after having considered all these factors can one engage in physical exercise without fearing any injury from it.

Charaka, another Indian doctor of the same period, advocated urinotherapy, drinking one's own urine or the "water of life" every morning to stimulate the regenerative functions of the body. The former Indian Prime Minister Morarji Desai, who took office at 81 and lived until he was 99, attributed the secret of his vitality to a regime of drinking his own urine in varying amounts every morning. The intestine knows and absorbs what is useful to the body while the remainder stagnates in the digestive tract where it acts as a purgative salt, attracting water and cleansing nerve fibers and intestinal muscle tissue. The taste of the urine is a valuable indicator of the state of the organism: when the body is not loaded with toxins, the taste of the urine is agreeable; if the body is loaded with toxins, its taste is unbearable.

MASSAGE

You lie down wearing only your shirt. Then the person giving the massage kneads the limbs one after the other almost as if he were kneading dough. He also pulls on the extremities of each limb, enough to crack all the joints in the wrists, the knees, and the fingers, without hurting you in the least since he does it so skillfully. . . . This work facilitates the circulation of fluids that the overbearing heat tends to make stagnate, causing them to no longer move freely. Massage makes the limbs more supple and nimble.

GUILLAUME LE GENTIL, 1770

In Kalaripayat, massage is first and foremost the science of the circulation of energy, and the creation of harmony in body, mind, and spirit. In Kerala villages, this therapeutic tradition is transmitted from generation to generation. All massage techniques fall under a general principle: the morning is suitable for tonifying, the evening is when you need to sedate and disperse. The treatments are given early in the morning during the monsoon season (July to November).

P. S. Balachandran points out that the massage techniques also take into account the patient's internal biological clock. For example, a heart patient is threatened between 11 a.m. and 1 p.m. Someone whose lungs are weak will be vulnerable between 3 and 5 a.m. The times indicated for the various organs are as follows:

*Fig. 4.2. Traditional massage
(as depicted in a historical document).*

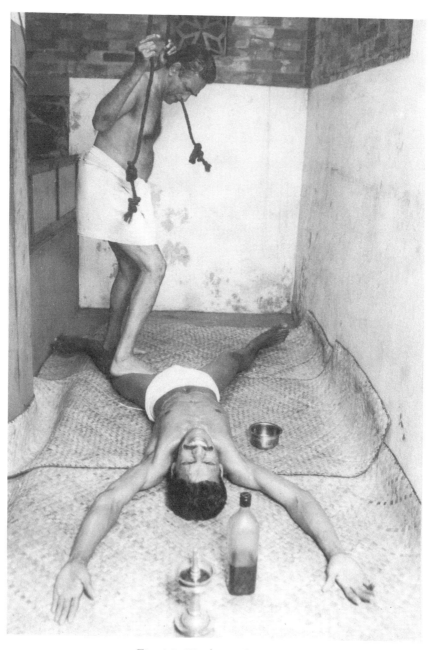

*Fig. 4.3. Traditional massage
(present day).*

- Between 1 and 3 a.m.—the liver
- Between 3 and 5 a.m.—the lungs
- Between 5 and 7 a.m.—the intestines
- Between 7 and 9 a.m.—the stomach
- Between 9 and 11 a.m.—the spleen
- Between 11 a.m. and 1 p.m.—the heart
- Between 1 and 3 p.m.—the intestines
- Between 3 and 5 p.m.—the bladder
- Between 5 and 7 p.m.—the kidneys
- Between 7 and 9 p.m.—the blood circulation
- Between 9 and 11 p.m.—the breathing functions
- Between 11 p.m. and 1 a.m.—the gallbladder

Massage acts on the skin, on the muscles, and on the internal organs by mainly treating pressure points and the vertebrae. It goes very deep.

Oil Massage

Coconut oil is clear and a beautiful yellow amber color. Its scent and taste are pleasant. When cooled it solidifies easily, becoming a brilliant white. Used as an external ointment it is very soothing, refreshing, and restorative. I used it myself to great advantage when treating external inflammations or light abrasions.

PIERRE BRUNET (1805)

Patients receive a deep massage with oils that bring a feeling of lightness to the body. The application of oil maintains the elasticity of body tissues and protects them from dehydration, especially in a hot and damp climate. According to the surgeon Sushruta, someone who has an oil treatment regularly will be less affected by difficult work or by accidental injury (sprain, fracture). He recommends an oil treatment every day since it maintains good nutrition of the tissues, brightens the complexion, strengthens the body, relieves fatigue, improves vision and sleep, slows aging, and prolongs life.

Sesame oil is invigorating and improves the quality of the skin, coconut oil refreshes and nourishes tissues, castor oil is very effective as an analgesic, liquefied butter has an anti-inflammatory action, animal fat reinforces muscles and joints, and bone marrow strengthens bony tissue.

The most used formulas of oils for massage are:

- *Mahasneha:* a mixture of sesame oil, liquefied butter, and animal fat or marrow. Being restorative, this mixture is often used for physical trauma.
- *Kuzhambu:* a mixture of sesame oil, liquefied butter, and castor oil in the following proportions: $\frac{1}{2}$, $\frac{1}{4}$, $\frac{1}{8}$. This preparation nourishes the tissues and reduces overheating during exercise.
- *Murivenna:* an oily, plant-based preparation, said to be good for healing wounds as well as for its anti-inflammatory and analgesic action.

Massage with the Feet

In the kalari, massage for the contestants can be traced back to the care given to warriors in former times. Massage shapes the fighter's body, which needs to be supple, lithe, and strong. The experience of the contestants themselves, enriched with contributions from ayurvedic practitioners, led to an education of masseurs that has been continued in the martial arts centers.

According to the ancient treatise of the great surgeon Sushruta, illness will not come near a body that has been well trained and has then undergone massage using the feet. Massage with the hands is for just one part of the body whereas massage using the feet is for the body as a whole.

Kalaripayat has developed a unique system of massage using the feet called *uzhichil*. Holding ropes attached to the ceiling framework, the masseur is better able to control the pressure of his feet on the body of the patient who is stretched out on the ground. The masters say that "Paradoxically one is gentler with the feet because they are stronger. In all physical exercise, one must never engage with all one's strength but *ardhasakttyaiva*, that is, only using half one's strength." The foot method is used with athletes from the age of 14 to 50, while massage with the hands is used only with more fragile subjects such as young children, women, the elderly, or someone who is ill.

Massages are given in series over seven days based on the strength or the needs of the fighter. The duration and depth of the massage is increased and decreased during each series. These massages are obligatory for students in martial arts and take place at least once a year for three consecutive years. When undergoing massage treatments, the patient has to follow certain rules of conduct: long rest periods, a bland diet with no saturated fats, sexual abstinence, and protection from cold and heat. This is done to avoid parasitic relationships.

The massage consists of continuous movement that flows like a dance and includes techniques of light touch, long gliding pressure in circles or ovals, along the body or across it, sometimes with traction that engages a muscle response, or using rubbing in one area or tapping.

With the upper and lower limbs the force of the massage is centrifugal (that is, pushing out from the center), whereas with the upper part of the trunk down to the navel the force is centripetal (that is, tending toward the center). The masseur is either treating knots, that is, parcels of cellulite in the skin that are painful to the touch, or deep areas of conjunctive tissue that surround the muscle fibers. Several massage techniques are used including rubbing, kneading, and percussive movements.

Massage with the feet is done according to the following sequence:

1. The subject sits opposite the masseur who pours oil into his right hand in order to rub it into the top of the subject's head, spreading it over the whole skull and then over the surface of the body.

2. Then the subject stretches out on a carpet and the masseur hangs from a rope attached to a rafter in the kalari, so that he can carefully control and regulate the pressure of his foot on the subject's body while standing on the other foot.

3. The masseur massages the back and sides, moving upward and then downward along the spine, ending gently at the coccyx. He works sideways on the muscles of the lower and upper part of the trunk, the back of the neck, the shoulders and shoulder blades, as well as the five lumbar vertebrae. The masseur uses small pulling maneuvers on the lumbar area and briskly rubs the buttocks and hips using a circular rubbing motion.

4. The masseur presses down and glides over the buttocks, down the leg, and back up again to the lumbar region and then down the other leg. The upper part of the knee is massaged with small circular movements. A sideways motion is used across the thighs. When moving up from the leg, the masseur may continue across the back even as far as the arm on the opposite side.

5. Starting from the shoulder, the masseur moves down along the arm and back up in a circular movement that includes the shoulder and the shoulder blade. This movement is continued across the back and down to the leg on the other side.

PRESSURE POINTS (*MARMAN*)

*Marman is a great art. You must not teach it to just
anyone. If you are considering teaching it to someone,
you must first of all examine your student in great
detail. Observe him and see what kind of a person he
is. Find out who he really is. Annoy him and see what
he says. Does he become angry or arrogant? Only after
you have put him to the test for a long time, will you
know if you can teach him what you know.*

PANICKAR GURUKKAL

One branch of ayurveda is minor surgery, which requires knowing
the body's pressure points or *marman*. According to a definition of
Sushruta these points indicate major concentrations of veins or nerves
as well as tendons and the principal nerve plexuses. Knowledge of
these vital centers—derived from observation of the human body
and of animals—is still taught today in ayurvedic schools and col-
leges that practice traditional Indian medicine.

Kalaripayat combatants must also be acquainted with them since
a blow to one of these sensitive points can induce a seriously debili-
tated state or death. In Kerala, the practitioners of Kalaripayat employ
this knowledge as a health-promoting art. One master corroborated
the significance of these vital points by showing me some techniques
of pressure on particular spots, producing effects that were astonishing and spectacular for a Westerner. He asked me not to write about
or reveal what I had seen and most particularly what I had felt. I
respect his wish to not have his secrets divulged.

In his treatise, known as the *Marma Sutras,* Sushruta gives a list
of 108 vulnerable body points classified into five categories: head and
neck (37), back (14), thorax (9), abdomen (4), upper and lower limbs
(44). There is also another classification based on the consequences

of hitting these points: nineteen of them produce immediate death, thirty-three death after a certain time, three death after the extraction of a foreign body, four produce paralysis or functional disablement, and eight cause violent pain.

An old Indian legend tells the story of a great lord who wanted to be assured of the efficacy of the methods he had been told so much about; he had no hesitation in sacrificing three thousand slaves in order to verify empirically the effectiveness of blows that were said to be fatal.

The primary dangerous pressure points are:

- *Thilaka varman:* forehead, between the eyes, where the eyebrows meet.
- *Aadi varman:* top of the skull; the first point to appear as a baby comes into the world.
- *Chenni marman:* temple.
- *Chevi kutti marman:* base of the ear.
- *Pidari marman:* base of the skull/cervical vertebrae.
- *Nakshatra kalam:* side of the eyes; fearsome point.
- *Nasimuna kalam:* base of the nose and tip of the nose.
- *Vettu varman:* point of the chin.
- *Chumayan kalam:* Adam's apple.
- *Surya adangal:* armpit.
- *Bhuja marman:* collarbone.
- *Neru marman:* solar plexus; one of the most dangerous because it's easy to hit.
- *Metha chuzhi kalam:* spinal column; three important points: at the beginning, in the middle, and at the end.
- *Padhakala kalam:* groin.

Each of these points can lead to serious injury but they can also be used to heal and promote health. Master Balachandran emphasized that "the art of these vulnerable points is at the service of noble causes and is not for the benefit of egoistic aims. This esoteric knowledge can also be used for aggression or murder, so the teaching of the marman is directed to disciples who will only use it for their own legitimate defense or against traitorous enemies."

He added: "The Nair were able to fight one hundred people at once and were able to hit with their gaze alone their adversaries' sensitive points. It was possible for them to hit the adversary from a distance using the projection of their internal energy and to wound him fatally if this energy reached certain vulnerable points on his body."

Using the Points

The man who has studied marman techniques and Kalaripayat is very useful to society. He must have certain character traits such as respect, civility, humility, patience, self-mastery, obedience, and kindness toward others.

He must be an example for everyone. This applies not only to men but also to women who also need to be like this.

Masters of this art and doctors mustn't ever harm others but only be of help to them. This is how they need to lead their lives.

There is one other thing you need to know. If some enemy comes to attack you, you first of all must remain quiet for a time. You must reflect calmly. This waiting time will relax your mind a little and this peacefulness in the mind is what is most important. In doing battle with an enemy who comes upon you, overpowering him or killing him is not what is most important. Anyone can do that. If, instead of doing battle with him, you say to your enemy, "You have won" as you bow before him, you will have accomplished the greatest feat in the world.

MADAVAN ASAN

The hand can be used as a sword, a club, or a lance. It can pierce, stun, knock out, cut, scratch, force, hook, whip, crush, grind, and fracture. The target point may be on the surface or may be situated deep within the body. The hand must know then how to measure the impact of the blow—its intensity, its precision, and how it is to be delivered. These factors will determine the seriousness of the trauma or wound that is inflicted. Training is required in order to develop sensitivity in the hand that is going to deliver the blow. Kalaripayat pays particular attention to the development of this sensitivity.

Within the body, there are openings through the muscle layers and there are fragile points in the bones. These vulnerability zones have been overlaid on the structure of the human body and pressure points naturally became evident to the warriors of antiquity as they fought. The vital areas are zones behind which a vital organ is functioning, like the heart, the liver, the spleen, the kidneys, or a major command center, as in the case of the nape of the neck or the temples. There are other vital areas in addition: the neck, the carotid artery, the thorax, the abdomen, the solar plexus, and the lumbar areas.

A part of the body may be vulnerable if it is densely vascular because there is then a risk of internal hemorrhage. The biological rhythms are related to the body's internal clock: certain times of day are more favorable than others for reaching certain pressure points. At highly enervated points, a blow doesn't cause any apparent damage but can unleash an inhibiting reflex that can

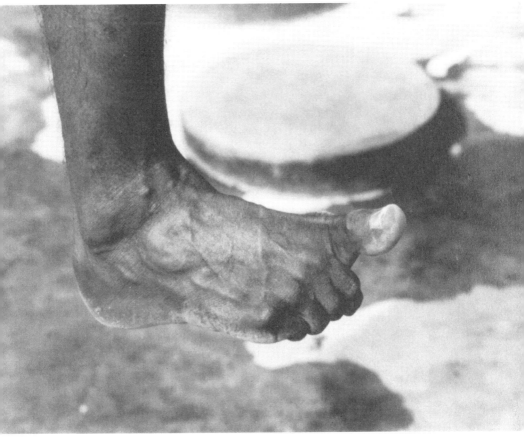

Fig. 4.4. Position of the big toe in striking pressure points.

cause blackout. Certain points create intense pain, then psychological shock; others can lead to paralysis of a limb or of a part of the body.

In the pressure-point science that has come down from the ancients on palm leaf manuscripts, the name of each pressure point is accompanied by an indication, a sort of code, on how to strike that point and what will ensue from doing so. Let us take as an example the thilaka varnam, the point between the eyes known as the "third eye," which the Indians mark with a red spot. A precise strike to this spot will cause the opponent to pass out and can also cause blood to flow into the mouth.

Resuscitation Technique

When a student loses consciousness because of a blow to one of these points, the master will sit him up against a wall while tapping slowly and repetitively on a specific pressure point at the top of the head.

In the full resuscitation technique, which is undertaken immediately following a loss of consciousness, pressure is used to stimulate a reflex area, which then resonates with nerve centers and with pulmonary and cardiac cycles. To perform this technique:

1. Place the man who has lost consciousness in a seated position. Hold him from behind with your hands on his pectoral area; his back should be held firmly upright by your knee placed between his shoulder blades.
2. Beat lightly and press strongly at the level of the fifth dorsal vertebra with the knee; at the same time bring his elbows together and pull them gently to the back to expand the upper part of the thoracic cage.
3. Next, induce an exhalation by pressing hard on the pectoral area.
4. This technique needs to be repeated until resuscitation is complete. The process can be finished off with shouts with varying degrees of intensity or sharpness in order to induce contractions of the cardiovascular system.

The Spread of Marman Knowledge

When Kalaripayat spread beyond the Indian subcontinent, it carried with it the concept of marman points as an essential element of martial arts. References to sensitive points are always found in

Asiatic combat sports whether they use weapons or not, and they are found also in Chinese acupuncture (energetic pathways and meridians),* as well as in Japanese resuscitation techniques. The masters examined their own bodies and found vulnerable points by experimenting on themselves with violent blows in order to discover the sensitivity of these points.

CLEANSING AND PURIFYING THE BODY

The *Gheranda Samhita* is a classic of hatha yoga written in the fifteenth century by Gheranda about whom very little is known. Kalaripayat masters often refer to body cleansing practiced by the Nair warriors in the sixteenth century. The techniques described by the Kalaripayat masters are similar to those described in the treatise by the sage Gheranda. They are also to be found in the ayurvedic medicine practiced in Kerala.

The information given here about these cleansing and purifying techniques is for the purpose of description only. It is inadequate to guide the safe performance of the techniques, which—if improperly done—can result in serious injury. In some cases the techniques stretch the limit of the imagination and appear to be legendary artifacts. The others, which appear possible for normal people, should be attempted only in the context of personal guidance and supervision of a Gurukkal, yoga master, or ayurvedic physician.

Cleansing: Dhauti

Four cleansing procedures are used to purify the body: cleansing of the stomach, *antardhauti;* cleansing of the buccal cavity, *dantadhauti;*

---

*Certain Kalaripayat masters use thin bamboo sticks, which they apply and hold in place on specific body points in order to heal their patients. This ancient technique known as *shalaka shastra* is the likely origin of acupuncture.

cleansing of the chest, *hrddhauti;* and cleansing of the rectum, *mulashodhana.*

Stomach Cleansing: *Antardhauti*

Stomach cleansing or *antardhauti* has four practices within it: purification using air, *vatasara;* purification using water, *varisara;* purification using the fire of vital energy called *agni, vahnisara;* expulsion of air through the anus, *bahiskrta.*

1. **Purification using air: *vatasara.*** In this technique the mouth is puckered up into the shape of a crow's beak and air is swallowed very slowly in order to fill up the stomach. The goal is to get the stomach moving so that the air is expelled through the bottom exit. This purification technique using air is really good and very secret. It purifies the body, gets rid of all sickness, and increases the fire element.

2. **Purification using water: *varisara.*** In this technique the mouth is filled with water up to the throat then the person swallows gently. The stomach is moved to form a hollow; the water is finally expelled through the anus. This procedure of using water to purify is also really good and very secret. It is said that a person who practices it zealously will obtain the body of a god: it will transform his impure body into a divine body.

3. **Purification using the heat of vital energy: *agnisara.*** In this practice the region around the navel is pulled back toward the spinal column one hundred times in succession. This yogic technique of purification through inner heat is said to bestow occult powers. It cures stomach ailments and increases the fire element in the intestines. It must be kept

secret and even the gods master it with difficulty. Using this *dhauti* alone it's definitely possible to obtain a divine body.

4. **Expulsion of air through the anus: *bahiskrta.*** The stomach is filled with air using the crow's beak gesture (*kakimudra*). The air is held in for an hour and a half then pushed out through the anus. This *dhauti* is still very secret and must not be revealed.

5. **Complementary cleansing.** Whoever is not able to hold the air in his stomach for an hour and a half (as in the technique above) will also not be able to master this great *dhauti* called "expelling downward." It is said that in this technique, the person immerses in water up to the navel and allows the rectum to come out (*shaktinadi*). The gut tubing is washed with the hand until there's nothing dirty left, then put back in place inside the abdomen. This purification is secret and even the gods master it with difficulty. Using only this method, a person can obtain an immutable divine body.

Cleansing the Buccal Cavity: *Dantahauti*

The purification of the buccal cavity, or *dantahauti*, is made of up four procedures: cleansing the base of the teeth, *dantamula;* purification of the base of the tongue, *jihvamula;* cleansing the auditory channels, *karnadhauti;* cleansing the cranial cavity, *karnarandhra.*

1. **Cleansing the base of the teeth: *dantamula.*** The base of the teeth is rubbed with acacia wood (the sap adds protection), or with purified clay until all impurities have been removed. Yogis consider this procedure to be one of the most important *dhauti* in yoga practice. It protects the teeth and makes them bright. It must be done daily. All yogis advise its use.

2. **Purification of the tongue:** *jihvamula.* Stretching the tongue makes a person able to overcome old age, death, and illness. It is done by reaching into the middle of the throat using three fingers—index, middle finger, and ring finger—and pulling on the root of the tongue. Then it is scratched very slowly. This allows disturbances in the phlegm to be cleared. The tongue should also be massaged at length with fresh butter and milk, after which this material is moved little by little toward the tip using a metallic instrument. This must be done carefully every day at sunrise and sunset. This daily task will lengthen the tongue.

3. **Cleansing the auditory channels:** *karnadhauti.* The two channels are cleaned out with the index or ring finger. Doing this procedure every day enables a person to hear the inner sound (*nada*).

4. **Cleansing the cranial cavity:** *karnarandbra.* The sinus hollow on the forehead (frontal sinus) is massaged with the thumb of the right hand. Repetition of this exercise helps ward off disturbances of phlegm. Through it the *nadi* are purified and clairvoyance is obtained. It must be practiced every day upon awakening, after meals, and in the evening.

Cleansing the Chest: Hraddhauti

This purification called *hraddhauti* includes three procedures:, cleansing with a rod, *dandadhauti;* cleansing by vomiting, *vamanad-hauti;* and cleansing using a cloth, *vasadhauti.*

1. **Cleansing with a rod:** *dandadhauti.* In this technique the stem of a plantain or curcuma (turmeric), or a reed is inserted into the esophagus, moved back and forth, and then slowly

removed. This kind of purification allows phlegm, bile, and excess moisture to be expelled through the mouth. All kinds of chest illnesses are cured this way.

2. **Cleansing by vomiting: *vamanadhauti.*** Two hours after each meal, enough water to fill the stomach up to the throat is drunk. Then, looking upward for a moment, the practitioner vomits up all the water. This daily practice terminates disorders of phlegm and bile.

3. **Cleansing using a cloth: *vasadhauti.*** A strip of cloth that is very fine and about four fingers wide is slowly swallowed, then withdrawn. This is called internal cleansing (*dhautikarman*). This technique cures chronic splenitis, fever, all diseases of the spleen, and leprosy. It gets rid of excess bile and phlegm. Whoever practices this technique will see daily improvement in health and increases in energy and well-being.

Cleansing of the Rectum: *Mulashodhana*

If the rectum is not purified the vital energy that moves down from excretion (*apana*) doesn't circulate properly. It is essential therefore to purify the rectum carefully with *mulashodhana*. Using a stick or the middle finger, it is important to repeatedly and in secret clean the rectum with water so as to get rid of bile. Practice of this purification enables a person to avoid constipation and combat dyspepsia or indigestion. Beauty and vigor are enhanced and the fire of the digestive system is stoked.

Enemas are also helpful to cleanse the rectum. There are two kinds of enema: in the one called *jalabasti* water is used, while the one called *shuskabasti* is dry. Enemas with water are carried out by getting into the water; the dry one is always done on the ground.

1. **Enemas with water:** *jalabasti.* While immersed in water up to the navel the person assumes the crouching posture termed "fury" (*utkatasana*) and then contracts and dilate the anus. *Jalabasti* stops urinary disorders, digestive difficulties, and pain that arises from disturbances of the element air. The body is rendered transparent just like that of Kama, the god of love.

2. **Dry enemas, on the ground:** *sthala or shuskabasti.* This dry enema is practiced in the posture called "rising toward the West," or *pashcimottana.* The stomach is slowly displaced backward, then the anus is contracted and dilated using the horse gesture, *ashvinimudra.* This practice helps to avoid constipation, increase the element fire in the intestines, and get rid of flatulence.

Purifications

Gheranda also lists other disciplines of purification, including: cleansing the nose, *neti;* churning the belly, *lauliki* or *laukiki;* the fixed look, *trataka;* and expectorations, *kapalabhati.*

Cleansing the Nose: Netikarman

Netikarman or "guiding the thread" is performed by introducing a fine, nine-inch-long cord into the nasal passage and then drawing it out through the mouth. Through the practice of this discipline a person can acquire the occult power called *khecari,* "moving in space." The practice cures disturbances in the phlegm and bestows divine vision.

Churning the Belly: Lauliki or Laukiki

Lauliki is performed by making a swirling motion with the muscles of the belly: they are pushed and moved rapidly in both directions.

Plates 1, 2, and 3. Kerala, a land with green fields of rice and bouquets of palm trees surrounded by lagoons and golden beaches.

Plate 4. Before practice, students apply oil in front of a picture of a goddess.

Plates 5 and 6. A typical training session.

Plate 7. Practicing a strike with the leg.

Plate 8. The low "on-guard" position.

Plate 9. Moving like water from the low "on-guard" position.

Plates 10 and 11. Bare-hands combat.

Plates 12 and 13. Fighting with staves.

Plate 14. Clubs used in hand to hand combat. ▶

Plate 17. Fighting with swords. ▶

Plates 15 and 16. Fighting with a dagger.

Plates 18 and 19.
Fighting with swords.

Plate 20. Using the eyes
in combat. ▶

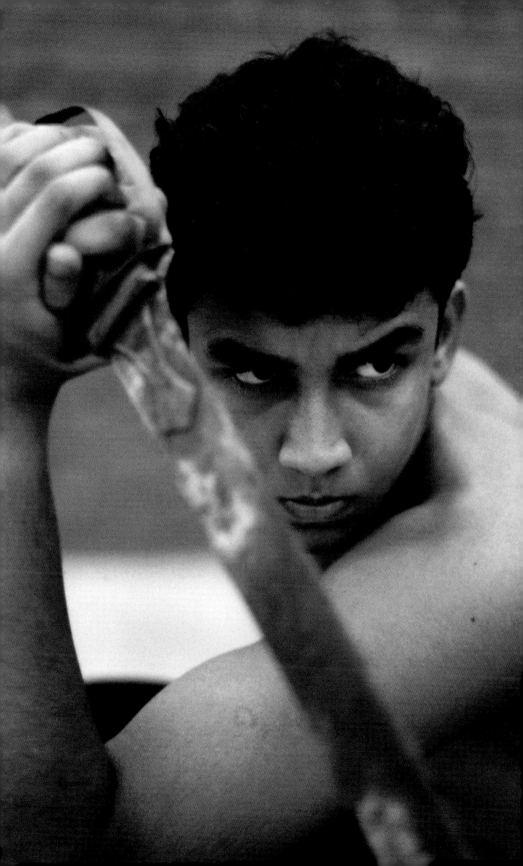

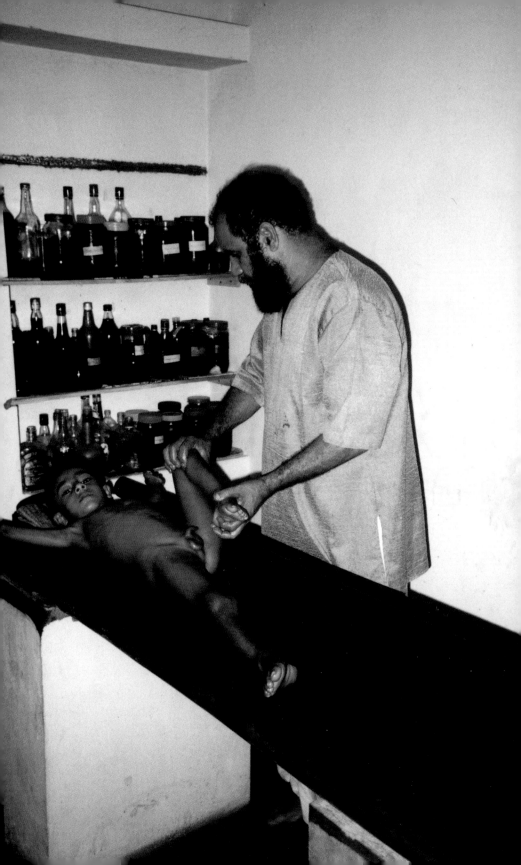

Plate 21. The Kalaripayat master is also a doctor.

Plates 22 and 23. A practitioner works on his breathwork techniques.

Plate 24. Practicing a quiet moment of meditation.

This destroys all sicknesses and increases the amount of fire element in the body.

The Fixed Look: *Trataka*

This practice is done by staring fixedly at a very small object without blinking until tears come to the eyes. The sages of old called it *trataka*. This technique will enable a person to acquire permanent mastery of "Shiva's consecration gesture," *shambhavimudra*. Eye disorders are cured and clairvoyance obtained.

Expectorations: *Kapalabhati*

Kapalabhati purification is done in three ways: *vamadrama*, "left-handed or pleasant way"; *vyutkrama*, "backward way"; and *shitkrama*, "fresh way." All of these practices prevent disturbances in the element phlegm.

1. **Left-handed:** *vamadrama.* Breath is drawn in through the left nostril to the lunar energy channel known as *ida nadi*, then breathed out through the right nostril through the solar energy channel known as *pingala nadi*. Then breath is brought in through the right nostril and breathed out through the left. The breathing in and the breathing out must be done without brusqueness but still pushing hard enough.

2. **Backward:** *vyutkrama.* Water is breathed in through the nose and expelled little by little through the mouth.

3. **Fresh way:** *shitkrama.* Water is breathed in through the mouth while the sound "sheet" is made, then expelled through the nostrils. This yogic practice makes the body transparent, like that of Kamadeva, the god of love. Old age never appears; suffering and decay will never overtake such a person.

FOOD

To lengthen thy life, lessen thy meals.

BENJAMIN FRANKLIN

*Our carnage shops, which we call butchers, where so
many cadavers are sold to nourish our own, would
spread a plague in India's climate. Such countries need
pure and refreshing food.*

VOLTAIRE

Since a mind cannot be pure if the body that houses it is not healthy, there are certain guidelines about eating that must be observed by the Kalaripayat practitioner. Also the nourishment derived from food underlies the proper functioning of the processes of life. Kalaripayat practice is done on an empty stomach either in the morning having eaten very little or in the evening before supper.

The Nair warriors were not vegetarian and had a predilection for fish. They ate very little meat, once a week at most—a regimen that modern Kalaripayat masters also advise. In order to avoid incompatibilities in the stomach, the Nair warrior would only eat one kind of food at each meal.

The staple Kerala diet includes rice and fruit as well as coconut, which is found everywhere throughout Kerala. Coconut contains significant amounts of vitamin E, which plays an important role in the battle with the free radicals that affect aging. Perhaps this is the secret that explains why the practitioners of Kalaripayat—who are avid consumers of coconut—also have lots of vitality. Everything is highly spiced: there's a saying that in northern India rice is eaten with chile and in southern India chile is eaten with rice.

As recommended also by ayurvedic medicine, Kalaripayat practitioners are taught to eat slowly so that the food can be properly chewed. Everything should be digested in the mouth before it is digested in the stomach. The more the food is chewed, the more nourishing it is; if it is chewed sufficiently, the amount eaten can sometimes be reduced up to half. Kalaripayat practice is done on an empty stomach, either in the morning or in the evening before supper.

An old Indian proverb says, "When you eat little, the stomach expands and good fortune shines on your life. Conversely, the more you eat, the more stuffed the stomach becomes and your life is affected by that. You should eat half of what you desire and drink one third of what would be your fill." It is interesting that these various recommendations, which are grounded in good sense, have been confirmed by recent medical advances.

Special Potions

Within the medicine that was practiced in Kalaripayat, there was a branch called *kaya kulp,* or the science of rejuvenation. Its principal discipline was *rasayana,* or the study of potions. The most common potion was called *soma,* an elixir that completely rejuvenated the body. In the mythological texts, soma was the juice of a plant that the gods drank to stay beyond the reach of death. It was visible only to the most pious and grateful of believers.

In the Kalaripayat tradition, soma was instead a mixture of ingredients; it contained asparagus, yam, dill, wild fennel, and ginkgo nuts, as well as one other ingredient that was kept secret. Only initiates had access to this potion. The text below describes a ritual that illustrates its action:

> The ill person is shut up in a room for seven days. He takes the
> soma. He vomits blood and his body swells up; worms crawl

out of different parts of his body, his hair and nails fall out, and his muscles shrivel. His organism throws off all accumulation of impurities and any vile substance. On the eighth day the rejuvenation begins: his nails and his hair grow back, his muscles regain their vitality, and his skin becomes ruby red. The new man is ready to spend ten thousand summers on earth in a new body.

BREATHING AND CARDIAC CONTROL

A conversation with Garnika Govindra provided invaluable details about the role of breath in the Kalaripayat tradition. He pointed out:

Life can be explained by the breathing cycle. Kalaripayat's breathing exercises take advantage of this principle by using an embryonic type of breathing. The individual can become perfectly sealed off, self-sufficient and impermeable. With success in establishing this inner circulation of vital essences, one breathes in a closed circuit just like a human embryo.

Breathing is the meeting place of physiological, psychological, and spiritual activity. The link or rigorous connection between mental activity and the breathing function is one of the important features of Kalaripayat. The science of breathing, known in India under the name of *pranayama,* and the techniques of hatha yoga called *asanas* play important roles in Kalaripayat, since controlled breathing leads to self-mastery and the *asanas* lead to great flexibility and to knowledge of the body.

Since the breathing function takes precedence over all other organ functions, there is always a connection between breathing and the mind in each organ's functioning. When all organ functions are suspended, the breathing is able to focus the mind's concentration on a single object.

There is always a connection between breathing and mental states. This implies that by breathing in a slower and slower cycle, it is possible to move into states of consciousness other than the state of normal waking consciousness. This breathing cycle is attained through a harmonization of three movements: breathing in, breathing out, and holding the breath.

The practitioner must inhale the air through his nose, filling the lungs completely. Then the air he has breathed is held and he counts his heartbeats. When he has counted one hundred beats, he must exhale the air through the mouth. In this breathing method, his ears must not hear the sound of breathing in or breathing out. Using a graduated practice, the practitioner must increase the amount of time the breath is held up to eight hundred heartbeats. . . . When an old man reaches this stage, he will be transformed into a young man.

Whoever wants to avoid passion and distractedness must learn to breathe, not with the throat alone, but with the whole body from the heels up. Only this deep, silent breathing refines and enriches one's substance. Moreover, this is the breathing that takes over during hibernation and also during ecstasy. When you breathe with the neck constricted or tense, you exhaust the breath and reduce its vivifying force to only its essential core.

The ultimate goal is to establish a kind of inner circulation of vital essences so that the individual can remain completely sealed off and survive the rigors of immersion unscathed. You become impermeable, self-sufficient, and invulnerable when you have acquired the art of nourishing yourself and breathing in a closed circuit as the human embryo does.

The practice of yoga is close to Kalaripayat and its breathing techniques. Everything is closely connected. They both produce an acuity and stability in the mind, and confer courage and patience as well as good health. (See plates 22 and 23 of the color insert.)

LONGEVITY AND IMMORTALITY

I could not bring myself to believe that Swany was almost eighty. He held himself as straight as a rod and he had the body of a competitive athlete. He was muscular and sinewy without an ounce of fat. His skin was as smooth as that of a thirty year old. He moved as gracefully and smoothly as a wild cat. Nothing escaped his bright, sharp eyes. . . . .

Swany introduced us to Mukesh, his nineteen year old student. Working with him, Swany gave us an impressive demonstration of adi khai pidutham: (control of your hands in strikes): blocks, parries, strikes that halt, getting up, and the marman techniques. Then, just as impressively, they performed training exercises and yoga exercises.

GERT J. LEMMENS
("KALARIPAYAT," *KARATE,* 1994)

As an "elixir of youth" or a "potion" for a fine old age, Kalaripayat, by means of its rigorous life discipline (both physical as well as spiritual) undeniably slows down the effects of old age: rheumatism, muscle degeneration, memory lapses, and brittle bones.

According to P. S. Balachandran, we human beings follow certain general patterns of growth and aging:

- At the age of twenty, the breath is at full strength and promotes bodily and mental activity.
- At forty, the breath circulates at maximum strength.
- At fifty, breathing becomes more difficult and the lungs no longer fill completely.
- At sixty, the blood vessels begin to change and arteries become constricted. Muscles become atrophied, the body begins to put on weight, repose is preferred over movement, while psychological aging sets in and intensifies.
- At eighty, energy slows down, especially in the lungs. The mind becomes cloudy and the body loses all flexibility.

"But for anyone who practices Kalaripayat regularly, this process is slowed down," explains Master Balachandran. He also divides existence into four seasons:

- During spring (childhood), the child learns the rules, learns how to pay attention, how to have patience, how to concentrate, how to know oneself and to live with oneself, and how to live with others.
- Summer, the age of the adult, is the season to come into one's own: clarity, endurance, humor, goodwill, and inner sincerity that is expressed outwardly. The young man knows who he is, he knows "who" his body is, he is master of his inner state, and he learns to be on his guard against vices: anger, women, wine, and greed.
- During autumn the mature man is fully conscious; he feels that he is coming into harmony not only with the deepest parts of himself but also with nature. His virtues are fairness, good-heartedness, and even-handedness. The mature man introduces action into his thought and thought into his action. His

attitudes and his behavior have given him a second nature; his conscious acts have become natural acts.

- Winter, the age of the old man, is the season of detachment, when harmony, felicity, virtue, tranquillity of body and mind, and the taste for contemplation come together. Man in his final season is close to perfection. He makes use of his mind like a mirror: if a bird is reflected in it, he displays a bird. The mirror reflects beauty as beauty, ugliness as ugliness. No stain tarnishes it. His mind has become like clear water that nothing disturbs deeply and his body is in harmony with his mind.

Indians don't have the same view of death that Westerners do. For them, it is like being born—a phenomenon of life leading from one state to another—and one of the natural consequences of the manifestation of existence. As we find in the Bhagavad Gita (one of the most studied philosophical texts in India), "the sage grieves neither for the dead nor the living." From the philosophical if not the medical point of view, the generally held belief is that since the universe and the human body are composed of the same substances or elements, it is their coming together that makes life. When, in old age, these elements become unbalanced, death follows, the death of the physical body.

The soul is considered to be one with the divine, one with the living force that created the universe, so the being himself is not destroyed by death but survives and will take up another body at the appropriate moment. All Indians have this innermost feeling and this allows them to attach little importance to the things of this world. Impermanence (everything that has a beginning must have an end) is one of the three characteristics of existence, a concept also developed by the Buddhists.

The Nair, like other Hindus, incinerate their bodies. Both the Vedic and Brahmanic religions prescribe the cremation of dead bodies. This cremation takes place in the open air, specifically near running water. Only wood is used for the fire. There is a complete funerary ritual to be followed by relatives and friends who join the priest. The bones are then gathered and placed in an earthenware urn that is buried in consecrated ground. The urn has a different shape depending on whether the deceased was a man or a woman. It's customary to place a small denomination coin in the dead person's mouth as token travel money for their journey to the Beyond. The son of the dead person, who actually should conduct the ceremony, breaks the cadaver's cranium with a hammer, so that it doesn't explode in the fire. Then those present circle the blaze three times, carrying the hammer in their left hand.

Formerly there was a special ritual during the cremation of a Kalaripayat master: his students-in-arms would make twenty-one turns around the fire as they made prostrations and chanted *Om gurave namaha:* "Oh, my master, I salute you." No doubt this ritual relates to the twenty-one Gurukkal chosen by Parasurama.

The habits that Indians have acquired work together wonderfully to maintain them in good health. . . . The custom of rubbing the whole body with oil remains it would seem an excellent remedy for all kinds of minor troubles and mishaps. . . . I won't even mention the suppleness that the oil affords to the limbs, which is such that they can assume all kinds of postures that look really painful and they can stay in them as long as they like. They move and turn around as if their bones were only tendons or cartilage and as if each one of their limbs had ten joints that open or close at will.

It is true that death takes it toll of all ages as it does everywhere else, but here mistakes are less frequent. You see few young people being buried unless they fell victim to some accident in particular.

You see men who seem made by nature as a measure of her intended length of human life. One whole century does not destroy them and these old men remain the proud possessors of all their organs and all their faculties right up until the moment they must finally pay the tribute that is exacted of all mortals.

I have seen many who had made their way through ten decades and who kept all the vigor of youth. I will mention only two who particularly struck me. The first remembered clearly all the events that had taken place in his country for a period of one hundred and four years. I found him very sensible, a great conversationalist, and very witty and cheerful. He had the bearing of a man of forty-five, powerfully built; his face was without a wrinkle and his complexion was good. He had not lost a single tooth nor one hair from a head of hair that was thick and almost all black, just like his beard and eyebrows.

I had him over for dinner. He ate as much as two ordinary middle-aged men and then returned to his village from which he had come in the morning, making in all a journey of a good four leagues (about twelve miles). What seemed to me most extraordinary about this was that this man was not an oddity because of his age, and so I concluded that his long life, which surprised no one, was not unheard of and that there were doubtless many others like him. . . .

One has to agree that this beautiful youthfulness is worthy of a right respect, because there can be no doubt that these venerable beings were accorded such a long career only because they lived in innocence while

exercising the virtue that guards the body from decay.
... By taking certain measures, such as hot drinks,
eating little in the evening, bathing often, keeping cool,
promoting perspiration, and above all avoiding excess,
one will enjoy health for a long time.

F. PERRIN, 1785

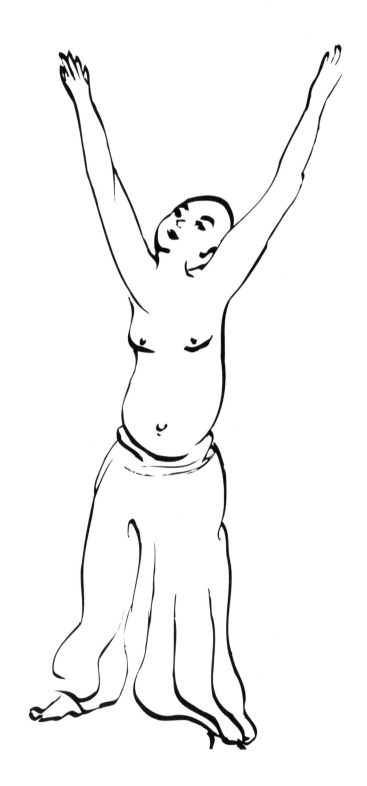

5

Kalaripayat and Other Cultural and Spiritual Traditions of Kerala

So long as you are not able to go beyond the mountain,
it will be impossible for you to reach the path.

TRADITIONAL FESTIVALS OF KERALA

The word *Kalaripayat* still evokes living terror in Kerala where legends and superstition abound. For example, there is the *kokkukarma,* the fearsome look that is able to stop an adversary, or the silent cry that immobilizes an attacker. Another technique is *uruloy,* or strangulation, using the cloth for wiping the body that the men of Kerala wear on their shoulder.

In the seventeenth and eighteenth centuries, the whole of Kerala society was steeped in a martial arts mentality, and in peaceful periods, tournaments were organized in which combatants sometimes died. In his *Letters from Malabar,* 1862, J. C. Visscher confirmed the existence of duels on a grand scale:

> There is a kind of sham combat still used in several kingdoms of Kerala. In these jousts or combats, hundreds, perhaps a thousand persons attack one another, armed with swords and shields, and inflict mutual wounds, sometimes indeed death.

At the present time various festivals or tournaments take place in Kerala, which maintain the martial spirit of the Nair. One example of this can be seen in the Occhira Kali, a festival that takes place in mid-June in the village of Occhira. The tournament is said to commemorate a famous battle between the forces of Travancore and those of the Raja* of Kayamkulam in 1734, a battle in which the Raja lost his life. Thi s tournament has a reputation for provoking heavy rainfall. This is almost always confirmed since the summer monsoon begins in this region starting at the beginning of the month of June. The local papers regularly publish a photo of the contestants with water up to their knees. The battle very explicitly ensures the rain.

The temple is consecrated to Parabrahma, and includes secondary sanctuaries for various other gods. To the south of this complex of sanctuaries, which are all open to the sky, there is a rectangular section of low-lying land oriented east–west that extends to the north-east of the sanctuaries as a kind of irregularly widened canal. This low-lying land and the canal is the *patanilam,* "the battlefield," where combat matches take place.

The participants come from two neighboring groups, east and west. They take up their positions on one side or other of this low-

---

*"King," a title taken by most Hindu chiefs who owned land prior to Independence.

lying land (to the east or to the west), armed with short canes or sticks. Then they run down the gentle slope en masse and confront each other in a series of duels, wielding their weapons in a technique that is close to the southern style of Kalaripayat. Some are clearly beginners (there are even quite young children), but others are experts.

The duels are engaged in a good-natured way with blows not forcefully applied and between participants who are at the same level of competence. When one of the duelists wins (the adversary falls or loses his weapon), he takes the other's stick as booty; the winners thus end up parading around with five or six sticks.

In former times, the tournament would have been practiced only by Nair in real battles with sword and slingshot. However, the serious accidents that arose from this practice led the government to outlaw the use of real weapons at the end of the nineteenth century. Travelers described the tournaments of the time in this way:

> There are tournaments in cities and villages, where the people dividing themselves into parties engage themselves in fight, some with wooden arrows, others without weapons but with bare hands, giving slaps on the face and punches in the belly.

Until very recent times, and in certain villages still today, bare-handed fighting has been the most widespread, at least in the center of Kerala. The technique is generally called *kayyamkali,* or "hand action." This is a kind of boxing that makes use of strikes with the right hand—held flat or using its cutting edge—while the left forearm is used to parry the opponent's blows. These pitched battles are specifically called *onattallu:* fisticuffs or brawls. Two halves of a community battle it out, often in rice paddies under the direction of a local chief. The battles take place between pairs of opponents or sometimes in groups.

FIRE WALKING

A fascinating account by Gilles Tarabout, *Sacrifier et donner à voir en pays Malabar* (*Sacrificing and Bringing to Light in Malabar Country*) (Paris: Ecole Française d'Extrême-Orient, 1986) describes fire walking in Kerala:

> . . . three tall conical piles of wood, made up of clubs and broken boards are erected along an east-west axis, facing the temple of Ganapati.* They are set on fire toward one in the morning, having been sprinkled with ashes consecrated by the oracle.
>
> After a few hours, only glowing coals remain, which are then spread out and smoothed down to form a roughly nine by twelve foot carpet.
>
> The crowd grows. About five in the morning the last dance sequence under the *pantal* ends. The *panakkarars,* headed by the oracle, move toward the pond, still dancing. They bathe in the water and then assemble again on the west side of the coals.
>
> The oracle throws consecrated ashes on the *panakkarars,* then, accompanied by two assistants, walks across the carpet of coals lengthwise, quickly but not running. Then the *panakkarars,* one by one, take their turns walking across, avoiding coals overturned by those who preceded them, coals that are indeed much hotter. Some go quickly, others really control their pace, walking with a confident stride at a normal speed. The crossing is accompanied by cymbals and the beating of drums.
>
> Walking across the coals is called *kanalattam.* . . . The walking is made possible thanks only to Bhagavati.† Bhagavati's power allows the fire-walkers to transcend what would otherwise be the

---

*The elephant-headed Hindu god, the son of Shiva and Parvati; he is the one who removes obstacles—based on this quality he has become a god of travelers.
†"She who is blessed," one of the many names given to the goddess Shakti (energy).

Fig. 5.2. An ancient representation of Kalaripayat from an illuminated manuscript now in the Musée Guimet, Paris.

inevitable course of events: to be seriously burnt if not completely consumed while walking across the coals. . . . The case of fire walking is illustrative; it is really a kind of miracle. The goddess makes it possible for her devotee, once properly purified by a preparatory discipline, to achieve what no one would be able to do ordinarily.

KALARIPAYAT AND *KATHAKALI*

As a precursor of Kerala traditions, Kalaripayat made many contributions to the development of well-known classical and rural art forms such as *kathakali* or *velakali* as well as numerous other popular traditions. Kathakali is an art that includes drama, décor, and music and is more than three centuries old. Its stories are inspired by the great epics and ancient sacred texts. The only form of expression not used by kathakali is the spoken word. The process of educating an actor in kathakali has borrowed a great deal from Kalaripayat in its methods of physical training and its choreography, a choreography in which the actor uses his body as a basic means of expression.

The first actors of the kathakali tradition were Nair warriors trained in the kalari. These actor-warriors changed Kalaripayat combat exercises, postures, step sequences, and so on to adapt them to the esthetic style of this dramatic dance form.

While kathakali is close to Kalaripayat because it uses its movements as gestures in drama, *velakali* is a kind of transposition of Kalaripayat into dance forms. It can be a transformation of the sacrifice found in battle, or it can be a type of allegory. In former times, only the Nair performed velakali as combat in the form of dance or a martial dance, using sword and shield and accompanied by an orchestra with cymbals, drums, horns, and oboes. The movements are based on rotations of the upper body, on knee bends that go progressively lower, and on rotations of the wrists with arms extended.

In his book *L'Inde des grand chemins* (*India's Major Pathways*) Jack Thieuloy very artfully brings to life this Indian art form:

Kathakali means "historical drama." Quintessentially Keralian, *Kathakali* is a play that's mimed and danced in the quivering light of lamps and candles set around the stage, so that shadows of the actors enhance the truly magical world that is evoked. With naked torsos, the tambourine players weave a slow, relentless enchantment. The story, which everyone knows, is not a modern author's text but is drawn from ancient Hindu epics and is dramatized by singers. All else is silence. And it is the silence that steals the show. How eloquent it is—the actors make up tableaux that simply vibrate with life.

In its workmanship and in the talent required, make-up becomes portrait art and the wings of the stage are turned into artists' ateliers. Artful too are the costumes and the coiffure. The faces become as complex and ornate as masks and the costumes are weirdly sumptuous and colorful. The make-up and the costumes are a strictly regulated language: the audience knows that a face painted green belongs to a character who is noble and good such as Krishna* or Rama.† If the green has saw-toothed patterns outlined in white, the noble character is arrogant. Bearded characters are demons and red beards are not the same as black beards, and so on. . . . All the actors are men who at some time will play women's roles.

These silent actors bring their characters to life using their whole body. Words and phrases are signals in gestures that

---

*The most venerated god in India. He is said to be the human incarnation of Vishnu in the third age of the world. He also symbolizes divine love, since he is the one who attracts.

†The solar incarnation of Vishnu, representing cosmic law. He brought happiness and peace during the second age.

are alive with meaning. Within these mudras [very similar to those used in Kalaripayat], the subtle movement of fingers and hands goes well beyond all metaphysics, all psychology, and all syntax that Western dramatists try to instill into their writing. Here, rolling the eyes in a figure eight distills a particular feeling; rolling them in a triangle a different feeling. Extending a little finger is more than adding opening quotation marks; a pursing of the lips is a superlative; raising a particular toe is the conditional; a special swivel of the hip is the subjunctive. But it's really more even than that because the tiniest gesture is quicker, more intense and more full of meaning than a whole phrase or even a paragraph and the body, being more communicative than speaking, speaks a multi-level language: the more skillful the mime, the more numerous the voices.

The intellectualized Western public in contrast rebels against this language. Being cerebral, dynamic, rational, and in a hurry, it prefers the alcohol of words where the oriental, being contemplative, religious, and visionary prefers the opium of gesture. The *Kathakali* dancers are mediums who take the spectator on a voyage out of himself, out of time, and out of this lower world in order to place him in communication with the absolute. In fact, *Kathakali* is so popular and its impact is so strong in the villages that I have no doubt that the Malayalam-speaking people, being politically astute, will one day bring the absolute down from heaven to reside on earth.

SPIRITUALITY AND MEDITATION

All Asian martial arts were developed in environments in which they were closely linked to religious and philosophical beliefs. In India, martial arts and meditation have always been especially closely connected. The practice of meditation, intended to transfer energy and the warrior's strength into a single point, is an integral part of the Kalaripayat master's teaching. (See plate 24 of the color insert.)

Some valuable insights are offered by the following selection translated from an anonymous Malayalam author:

> Up to the seventeenth century, Kalaripayat was one of the factors that contributed to the spiritual unity of Kerala. All religious movements, all practices involving magic, all popular mystical movements assimilated the principles of Kalaripayat. This assimilation took place to a different extent depending on the inner needs of each popular religious or mystical movement, but no spiritual movement in this area of India was able to remain apart from Kalaripayat.
>
> Kalaripayat was an effective tool of spiritual conquest and was connected to the expansion of Buddhism. An Asian technique first and foremost, Kalaripayat was assimilated in all areas of Asia and adapted itself locally in each one of them.
>
> Kalaripayat had a great assimilation capacity and absorbed innumerable local magical and mystical practices which it encountered in the path of its expansion.
>
> These techniques of physiology and meditation were adopted by monks in China and then penetrated also into the Zen monasteries of Japan. Wherever Buddhist forms of Indian spirituality spread, Kalaripayat techniques were transmitted as well.
>
> The history of Kalaripayat practices is in fact the history of the conflict between mysticism and asceticism, between contemplation and meditation, between combat and non-violence. As techniques of spiritual independence, Kalaripayat practices could be agents of the soul's isolation or they could equally well be vehicles for union and fusion.
>
> Meditation, which is important in Kalaripayat, also has a value as magic: Through meditation one assimilates, dominates,

or possesses the object of the meditation. Through meditation the objective laws that determine the physical universe can be suspended. The practitioner can intervene in the universe, modify reality, or invalidate any objective law. The world of combat is very far from this.

From all of this, we can recognize a courageous magical construct that is implied by Indian spirituality in the way it brings things together, but rarely is this spirituality able to develop further in a definitive way. In Kalaripayat, meditation presumes a continuous universe, a vast field of forces in which the will of man can act at a distance and modify the way things are. The universe is a vast fabric imbued with energy and any individual existence that finds itself in the framework of this immense receptacle of forms is in direct contact with the whole of the universe.

But this eternal return to the universe, this infinite cycle of reincarnations is in fact the infinite prolongation of larval existence that implies death rather than life. Because for all Indian spirituality the human condition is tragic: man can be neither happy nor free; the life he leads on earth is the life of a larva since he lacks spiritual independence and a state of grace, the necessary conditions to exist in reality. We might even say that *karma**plays the roll of a "hell." Just as in other religions men go to hell for their bad deeds, in India they return to earth, reborn into the human condition according to their own karma.

For Indians in general, living mechanically in ignorance is to be living the life of a larva, a life of torture. The aspiration of the Indian soul to rise above the human condition, to a state of grace and independence, is the same as the desire to avoid hell—that is, the terrible

---

*In Hindu and Buddhist philosophy *karma* is the law of action that determines how each action or thought produces its effects on the spiritual totality of the being, and therefore influences his cosmic becoming, as well as determining his future incarnations.

life of a larva that is in fact what earthly existence amounts to.

Kalaripayat's magic character is born out also by the importance that it accords to the practice of meditative techniques and to the act of meditation, since, by acting in this way, man can save himself using his own resources. It needs to be said that this orientation through the practice of meditative techniques implies something else as well: it indicates a tendency to be practical and connected to experience, a tendency that is seen in numerous religious reforms and mystical techniques in India. We have been able to see how deeply rooted this spiritual attitude is in India.

Mystical forms are to be found in all local worship in India, a worship that is most often organized around goddesses. The mixing of mystery and magic, of combat and life, and of the struggles among the spiritual framework that dominates all of Indian life are illustrated nowhere more clearly than in Kalaripayat practices.

Kalaripayat practices have their origins in the civilization of Kerala but they have been influenced by the Indo-Aryan magical paradigm of sacrifice: suspending the breathing corresponds to a ritual movement inward.

Kalaripayat is acquiring more and more pronounced mystical values and is also becoming a very complex spiritual technique in which union with God is achieved by means of a mystical physiology. Mystical physiology is the greatest experiential practicality that can actually be achieved through Indian spirituality. This essentially mystical and experiential practicality corresponds to what is metaphysically real—the same perfected self-sufficiency and spiritual grace sought by other Indian philosophies.

Whereas, at certain times in history, the metaphysically real, self-sufficiency and spiritual grace acquired through knowledge have appeared too abstract, too artificially structured and rigid, Kalaripayat could always satisfy any spiritual need: engaging in Kalaripayat would lead to ecstasy, to fulfillment, and to mystical grace and therefore to victory over oneself. By going completely beyond the human condition, by burning up all varieties of passion, pain, and human concepts, one could accomplish a perfected existence and the most complete spiritual independence.

For the Indian spirituality that hungers for an absolute and palpable freedom, death is various and dramatic. It is a sequence of states and of experiences whereas the life of the real is unique, eternal, independent, and conscious. The human condition— being in slavery and ignorance—is in fact a perpetual death. The life of the real can only be the highest degree of freedom in consciousness and grace, which is to say that it really means attaining Nirvana.* We conquer this eternal and beatific life by going beyond the human condition and by suppressing the roots that nourishes that condition. We are liberated from death in dying. Kalaripayat allows us to come to this freedom.

LEGENDS AND TALES OF KALARIPAYAT

Here are a few stories and legends drawn from the oral tradition that illustrate the spirit of Kalaripayat. These symbolic stories clearly need to be viewed from within the storyteller's cultural context.

Loyalty to the Master
(Guruvinuvendi yudham cheyuka)

About four hundred years ago, there was a courageous and loyal warrior from Malabar called Iravi Kutti Pillai. He practiced Kalaripayat and knew the most secret weapon techniques.

---

*Nirvana is the supreme state of non-existence and non-reincarnation, and of the integration of the being. It is not nothingness, but rather the state of absolute purity that allows the soul to become integrated into the cosmos. In Buddhist philosophy it is more specifically represented as the extinction of the three passions: desire, hatred, and ignorance.

Fig. 5.3. An ancient representation of Kalaripayat from an illuminated manuscript now in the Musée Guimet, Paris.

He was the head of an important clan from the south of the country at a time when Tamil from the Damila tribe attacked his lands. With other warriors who were his friends he mounted a resistance, but the fighting was so fierce that his friends abandoned him in a cowardly way. Overwhelmed by the number of his enemies, he died in battle from a sword blow that severed his head. Since his head had symbolic value, it was offered to the Tamil king by the Damila tribe. His headless body was sent back to his family so that funeral rites could be performed.

Kali Nair, a disciple of this master warrior, who unfortunately wasn't with him during the battle, became very angry about the decapitated body. He swore to Kutti Pillai's mother that he would bring her son's head back to her. How could funeral services be held for a man without his head?

Armed with his urimi around his belt, he left alone on horseback to wrest back his master's head from the Tamil. He had to battle alone courageously and killed many warriors of the Damila tribe. When the king was informed of this, he ordered his men to cease fighting and had this fearless man brought to him. When Kali Nair—who had the courage to attack a whole army single-handed—was shown into the presence of the king, he was received with honor for fighting valiantly with no fear of death. The king ordered that his master's head be returned to him since he was loyal and faithful. He soon became the head of his own country.

Even if the enemy is impressive, the Nair soldier must be loyal toward his country and must fight for his master.

Being a Master
(Kalaripayattu Cheyunna Sthree)

There was once a woman practitioner of Kalaripayat who was expert in the use of the ottakol, *a weapon made of wood that makes it possible* to strike the adversary's vital body points very precisely. She was called Unniyarcha and lived in the north of the country of Malabar around the eleventh century.

One day she was traveling on horseback with one of her women disciples to the temple of Ganesh (the elephant-headed god of India) for a marriage celebration. Since her destination was far away, Unniyarcha had to cross mountains and forests. In a forest on route they were surrounded by bandits who wanted to steal from them. Unniyarcha defended herself against the bandits using her ottakol. After a furious battle all the bandits were disabled but still alive; Unniyarcha had a great respect for life. The leader of the bandits was so impressed by the courage and force of this woman that he became a loyal disciple and thereafter never left her side.

Another day she was attacked in the woods by a pack of wolves. She continued on her way without losing her composure, her face resolute and so impregnated with explosive force that the animals froze in their tracks; she was able to pass right through the middle of the pack unscathed.

The tale is also told that on another occasion Unniyarcha accepted the challenge of a master who wanted to measure his skills against hers. The encounter took place on a beach with strong sunlight beating down. It is said that Unniyarcha simply raised her sword at the right moment, reflecting the sunlight directly into her opponent's eyes, and in this way won the battle.

Being Humble
(Guruvum Shishyanum)

A long time ago, a man who was called Lakshmi came to see a master and asked him to teach him Kalaripayat. After taking stock of his future student, the guru agreed to teach him this martial art.

After six months of practice, the guru asked his student how many opponents he could fight and defeat. The student replied, "Ten opponents."

After a year the master asked the same question and the student replied, "Five opponents."

After five years, the guru once again asked the same question. The student replied, "Almost no one."

After years of study, we always discover that there are many things we don't know.

Courage and Honor
(Abhimanam)

Velu Thampi Dalawa was a Nair warrior who fought for the liberation of India. He was also a minister of the King of Travancore in 1820.

The English at this time had levied a tax on the coconut harvest. Velu Thampi Dalawa did not accept this unfair tax and led a revolt. The English were attacked during the night. There was a battle with extensive losses on both sides, and the English, because of their fire-arms, were victorious.

Velu Thampi Dalawa and his younger brother were surrounded in a temple. Seeing that there was no way out except to be taken prisoner, he asked his brother to kill him. His brother refused. Velu Thampi Dalawa then committed suicide, using his own sword. His death was an affirming demonstration of force and will. The English invaded the temple and discovered the dead body of this courageous Nair leader. They hung the body in the center of the town to impress the population. Velu Thampi Dalawa became a martyr and a symbol of resistance to the enemy.

His statue is to be found today at the very spot where he was hung in Trivandrum, the capital of Kerala.

6

The Kalaripayat Way of Life

Real knowledge comes from within. He who knows what is right will do what is right.

THE MEETING: MADRAS, 1994

When a man wants to express what he thinks he has understood, he becomes incapable and his words imprison him.

My guide, Jesus, wants me to visit an old Kalaripayat master who is also a master of yoga breathing and meditation. "An astonishing person, a sage," he tells me. An appointment is arranged for me.

The house is at the end of a dusty street teeming with children as they always are in India—a street with indescribable odors, bitter, unsavory yet suddenly rather sensual. On one side of the road, shacks and their beggars line the route.

I push open a heavy door and an old woman comes toward me, bowing repeatedly, offering words of welcome that Jesus translates for me. She leads me through a dark corridor to the living room that looks out on a garden burgeoning with luxurious vegetation including jackfruit trees and bougainvillea.

A door opens slowly. The old master, aristocratic, with haughty bearing, who is called Pratap, appears and leads us to a large, empty room furnished only with a carpet.

"Have a seat," he says, indicating the carpet.

With a supple movement, he is quickly seated and there we are both crouched down in the hot, muggy atmosphere of the room. After offering a few polite words, I explain the reason for my visit, my interest in Kalaripayat and my research on the martial art and its different techniques.

He looks at me with a slight smile, his eyes twinkling. In spite of his advanced age, his look is amazingly lively. His body seems lithe and muscular.

"How can I can help you?"

He speaks perfect English, a result of the British occupation. On a kind of wooden stand where incense is burning, filling the room with its penetrating scent, palm leaf manuscripts arouse my curiosity. The master hands one to me and explains, "I write these at night. They are texts that summarize my experience with our art. Some young people who like to call themselves my disciples often come here to read them."

After a few minutes, the old woman returns with a pot of boiling tea, bananas, mangos, and coconut.

We have our tea spiced with cardamom and chat while enjoying the fruit. He shows me other documents, several centuries old he tells me, which have been handed down from generation to generation. Written by hand on palm leaves and illustrated with finely engraved diagrams, these documents deal with astrology, medical science, pressure points, and the art of combat. They are written in the Malayalam language (a Dravidian language of south India) and are anonymous: *Parappa Padu Varman Pandirndum, Pankanam Todu Maram Thonutiaarun*. Some of them show animals like lions, monkey, and serpents in combat.

Pratap then tells me about the origins of his art and how the great masters observed the combat techniques of animals:

"Kalaripayat proceeds from two great principles: the mind is in charge in the body, and one's opponent is vanquished by turning his own force back on him. The swallow swoops down to peck, the bear grabs, the serpent undulates, the crane spreads his wings and pecks with his beak. The masters of former times, having withdrawn to the solitude of the mountains to live in harmony with nature and to meditate, studied and observed the movements of various animals and from these creatures they learned their main defense and attack positions."

I steer the conversation toward meditation and the breathing practices that the masters deem so important and that they so carefully guard in secrecy. He stops me immediately, saying that he is not allowed to speak to me about that. I insist. After a long moment of silence, he agrees to tell me a few details about certain theories underlying the breathing techniques.

"Nature has set at twenty-one thousand the number of our exchanges of breath (in-breath and out-breath) between two sunrises. A breathing cycle that is too quick, or is noisy and agitated, accelerates this rhythm and shortens the length of one's life. A slow, deep and calm rhythm economizes on what we have been allotted and lengthens the life. Exchanges that have been economized in this way accumulate and form an important reserve from which a man can extract several extra years of life.

"Those who are advanced in the art of Kalaripayat and in meditation breathe more slowly than do ordinary mortals and encounter nothing uncomfortable in doing so. Our masters have the key to the breathing process. They know that the circulation of blood and breathing are closely connected. They also know that the mind is directly related to the breathing and therefore that it knows the secret of awakening spiritual consciousness by acting on the breathing.

"It should also be noted that the breath is only the physical expression of a more subtle force that is the real underlying support for the body. It is the energy that is hidden and is invisible in all our vital organs. When it departs from the body, breathing stops and that is what we call death.

"Controlling the breathing allows us to master, to a certain extent, this invisible flux. However, even though we push the control of the body to the extreme so that even movements of the heart can be mastered, don't imagine that our former masters were only thinking of the body and its organs when they began to teach our system."

I listen. He is quiet for a few moments.

"Can you really control the working of the heart?"

"Yes, our vital organs, the heart, the stomach, the kidneys, are brought under control to a certain degree by our masters."

"How is that done?"

"By the action of mental processes, combined with the appropriate exercises. Of course, these are part of the higher levels of Kalaripayat practice. They are very difficult and few adepts manage to do them the way they need to be done. Thanks to these practices, I have been able to control, up to a certain point, the cardiac muscles and also the other organs. Here, put your hand on my wrist and feel my pulse."

As he says this, the old man assumes a lotuslike posture, lowers his head, and closes his eyes. His breathing becomes slower and is soon imperceptible. Silence gathers in the room. I wait for a few minutes, noticing nothing unusual. His heart is beating at about sixty beats a minute.

Then, gradually, I feel the heartbeat slow down, become slower, then slower still until it comes down to about forty beats per minute.

This phenomena lasts about a minute, then gradually the heart-beat speeds up and returns to its normal rhythm.

After a few minutes, he opens his eyes. He seems tired.

"Did you feel it? That was nothing compared to what my master was capable of. He could isolate an artery and stop the blood flow in it. Here, I'll show you something else. Put your hand under my nostrils."

I obey. I feel the warm air of his out-breath on my skin. He closes his eyes and becomes very still, motionless as a marble statue. He enters an ecstatic state. Little by little his breathing diminishes, then stops. I watch his nostrils, his lips, his shoulders, his thorax: no movement, no exterior sign of breathing. He remains for several minutes in this nearly cataleptic state. When Pratap emerges from this state, he explains:

"This stopping of the breathing is only allowed for adepts who are already advanced in their practice. An elephant breathes much more slowly than a monkey. The elephant also lives longer and it's the same for certain big reptiles: there is a relationship between the function of breathing and longevity. In the Himalayas, you find bats that sleep for the whole winter. They remain for months hanging from the ceiling of mountain caves and their breathing stops completely until they awaken. Mountain bears are as stiff as cadavers during their winter hibernation and their breathing is also suspended. Why would you think that man couldn't achieve what animals do as a matter of course?"

He then explained that according to him there are three ways of achieving this:

- The first consists of practicing breathing exercises every day. This practice must be perfected under the direction of a master who is capable of demonstrating with his own body how the teaching is to be carried out.
- The second consists in taking regularly certain rare herbs

cultivated by only a few great adepts who know about them. Ayurvedic medicine uses these herbs. When his time comes to depart from this world, the Gurukkal chooses from among his disciples one whom he considers to be the most worthy and he reveals to him the secret of these herbs. In the future, this disciple will be the only one to possess this knowledge.

- The third is more difficult to explain. In the brain there is a small cavity that is the seat of the soul. A kind of membranelike valve subtly prevents entry to it. At the base of the dorsal spine arises a vital fluid. The continuous outflow of this fluid is the cause of aging; controlling it is, on the other hand, a source of life.

Pratap continues: "When a man has acquired complete mastery of himself, he can begin to exercise this control through a series of practices. If he manages to have this fluid move up into the upper part of the spinal marrow, he then needs to try to concentrate it in that cavity in the brain, but a master has to help him open the protective valve. If a master agrees to this, this vital fluid will enter the cavity and will act as an elixir of longevity. It is impossible to achieve this alone. Someone who succeeds in doing it can meet all the conditions of an apparent death and outwit the death that seeks him out. This means that he can choose the moment of his death.

"A man who has these three methods available to him can live in good health for a very long time."

I am reminded of an account I had discovered in my research. Written in 1804 by Dr. Pierre Brunet of Mangalore, it was titled *Voyage à l'Ile de France, en Inde et en Angleterre* (A Voyage to the Paris Region, India, and England):

According to the statements of his friends and all his acquaintances, this man, at the time I knew him, was managing to live on a very small quantity of rice, an amount that he kept reducing further every day. He never spoke and made responses only in writing. He knew several languages, English among others. He was tall, thin and healthy looking. He was then 61 years old. He slept only one hour a day and spent the rest of the night in contemplation, seated Malabar style, that is on the ground, with his legs crossed, his hands on his knees and his fingers extended with the thumb and index fingers curved together.

After having assumed this posture, he entered a state of ecstasy and gave no sign of movement or of breathing. His eyes remained open without the slightest blinking, and after a few moments tears trickled from his eyelids. I saw him myself in this state at the request of his friends who had spoken to me about it and which I had trouble believing. He stayed like that for about half an hour. It hurt me to see him motionless like that. Just as he had entered only gradually into a state of ecstasy, he also left it in stages and what seemed to me especially odd was that he seemed embarrassed to return from it.

We noticed that in this state he was aware and heard accurately everything we were saying. I learned from him that he had only acquired this custom during the past few years. From his companions I learned that he had learned his secret from another Brahmin; that he had suffered greatly in achieving this mastery; that it had been ten years that he no longer spoke, no longer ate fish or curry, and no longer had intimate relations with a woman; that earlier he had spent several years purifying his body using salt, spices and lotions, a process that provoked serious illness and from which he had greatly suffered.

He stated that if I wanted to remain in India, take his place and promise to follow all his instructions, he would tell me his secret and all the benefits that had flowed from it. Having been a general's chief servant he had enjoyed some of life's delights, but nothing could equal the pure and real pleasure that he experienced in his ordinary contemplation. He compared his rapture to that of a man who possesses for the first time a woman he has desired for a long time and who responds to his affection, or to the intoxication experienced by someone who has consumed an alcoholic drink or an opiate that has induced an ecstatic state while still in possession of his faculties.

When I asked him why so few of his compatriots enjoyed this level of happiness, a level that led to immortality, he replied, as always in written form, that it was "because there were very few men who were willing to give up the ordinary, every-day pleasures of life, and undergo so many privations in order to adopt a purely spiritual and contemplative life."

In the course of other conversations with him, I had the impression that he had meditated deeply on several metaphysical topics. He said that he had looked into and studied most of the current religions, and from all this study only one truth emerged for him, which was the knowledge of a single God who directed the universe and made himself known to man through his handiwork and the laws of nature. He considered his religion to be the oldest one on earth and that it had given rise to all other religions both in Asia and in Europe. He went on about this for some time. He would have continued longer if his companions had understood him more or if they had had the patience to continue interpreting for me. What he told me was in harmony with the principles and history of the Brahmins of Benares.

Whatever the case may be regarding his presumptions and opinions, this man, who meditated a great deal, certainly had a talent for knowing others, understanding how to appreciate them, ascertaining their tastes and how they were. Like a second Socrates, he was forewarned about disgrace having befallen his friends or about ill will in those who wanted to hurt him. When he went to see someone, he knew ahead of time, or it would come to him on the way there that he was going to meet that person. All the Indians belonging to the caste of this Malabari held him in great veneration. They considered him to be a privileged being, like a saint whom they thought would never have to die. They all seemed in agreement about that and were also completely convinced that there were people among them who achieve immortality and who are always alive helping everyone else. In brief, I observed surprising things in this man, both from the physical point of view and concerning his character. I have set all this forth as established facts: I believe that my observations have been accurate and I leave their explanation to the European philosophers.

Pratap shares with me the following explanation found in a book by Kamalashila, a Buddhist monk who traveled to Tibet in 749 to establish a monastery there, and who wrote numerous books on Buddhist doctrine.

If it is not maintained, the body is like a pile of foam: you can't pick it up and its five desires cannot be satisfied. Like a river that is rushing toward the ocean, the body quickly comes to old age, sickness and death. Like manure, people leave it behind in disgust. Like a town made of sand that the wind carries away in the twinkling of an eye, like an outlying country where you see a multitude of enemies, like a dangerous road, the body constantly distances itself from the true law. Like a tall house founded by the one hundred and eight desires, like a leaky vase that water constantly escapes from, like a richly painted vase that has been filled with garbage, like a stagnant canal, the body is always full of waste and impurities. Like an illusory dream, the body leads stupid men astray and prevents them from knowing truth. Like a faded flower, the body quickly comes to old age and feebleness.

Like a chariot, the body travels in the company of death. Like the dew, the body cannot last long. Like a house, the body is inhabited by four hundred and four illnesses. Like a trunk where a venomous snake is living, like a butterfly who sees the flame and burns up in it, like a conquered kingdom with eighteen traitorous kings, like a banana palm that has no strength or solidity, like a shipwrecked vessel, the sixty-two heresies lead it astray. Like a tumble-down pavilion that has lost its former beauty, like a guitar whose strings give forth hopeless sounds, like a drum covered with hide and wood and whose inside is empty, like a vase of dried clay, the body has neither consistency nor firmness. Like a city made of ash that is carried away by wind and rain, the body quickly comes to old age, illness and death.

"Listen to another old Indian tale," continues Patrap, translating one of his old documents:

Once upon a time there was a man who was crossing the desert and who found himself being pursued by an enraged elephant. He was seized with terror and had no idea where he could hide when he noticed a dry pit near some tree roots. He grabbed onto the roots and lowered himself into the pit. But there were two rats, one black and one white, who were both gnawing away at the roots of the tree. At the four corners of this tree, there were four venomous snakes trying to bite him and underneath a dragon loaded with poison. In the depths of his heart, he feared the venom of the dragon and the snakes and the breaking up of the roots. There was a swarm of bees on the tree, which dropped five drops of honey into his mouth: but the tree shook, the remainder of the honey fell to the ground, and the bees stung the man. Then a fire suddenly came and burnt up the tree.

The tree and the desert stand for the long night of ignorance.

*Fig. 6.2. The Gurukkal and his students start their training
with religious rituals.*

- *The master then goes to his dispensary behind the kalari
  where his patients await him. He becomes a doctor
  who brings relief and healing, practicing massage and
  dispensing herbal remedies until 11 a.m.*
- *Next he prepares his different oils.*
- *This is followed by lunch and rest until 3 p.m.*
- *Then more consultations until 5 p.m.*
- *From 5 until 7:30 p.m., training in combat with his
  students.*
- *This is followed by meditation, a light meal, and the
  reading of sacred texts. The day ends around 9 p.m.*

The man stands for the heretics. The elephant stands for the instability of things. The pit stands for the shore between life and death. The roots of the tree stand for human life. The black rat and the white rat stand for day and night. The roots of the tree, gnawed at by these two animals, stand for forgetting ourselves and the erasing of all thought. The four venomous snakes stand for the four great things (earth, fire, water, and wind). The honey stands for the five desires (love, music, perfume, taste, and touch). The bees stand for vicious thoughts. The fire stands for old age and illness. The poisonous dragon stands for death.

From this, we see that life and death, old age and illness are extremely fearsome. We need to constantly have this thought penetrate us and not allow ourselves to be assailed and dominated by the five desires.

Pratap is quiet for a few moments, then concludes: "Everyone would like to be able to defy death, but do not forget: applying this system is dangerous. Also, don't be surprised that our masters keep certain practices secret as you would with a precious gem. You have to learn to walk before you learn to run, but this is difficult for Westerners to understand."

Outside, the bright pink of the bougainvilleas suddenly darkens and they seem almost red. Night falls abruptly as it often does in this part of India. When the darkness begins finally to creep into the room, the master lights a *dipa* (oil lamp), which he hangs from the ceiling. Incense still fills the room with its mystical perfume.

Pratap continues, "The control of the body must go hand in hand with the control of the mind; the first does no more, in truth, than to prepare the way for the second. When our sages of former times received the doctrine from the hands of Parasurama, they understood that the conquest of the body was only the first step toward the conquest of the mind and that this second conquest was only a movement toward divine perfection. So that is Kalaripayat."

He falls silent. Under the dim light of the lamp, his face seems transformed. He concludes: "The master is he who dissipates darkness."

A KALARIPAYAT MASTER'S DAY

In spite of the troubled modern world all around him, the life of a Kalaripayat master has not changed in hundreds of years. There is a strict daily regimen much like that of monks in a monastery.

- The master rises at 4 a.m. to clean and prepare the kalari.
- He makes a ritual offering of flowers on the puttara, the corner altar, for the various gods.
- After bathing the master will meditate for thirty or forty minutes in order to prepare mind and spirit.
- At 6:30 his students arrive, and up to 8:30 they train and practice Kalaripayat techniques in the kalari.

The following day will be the same, punctuated perhaps by the arrival of the monsoon, which slows life down a little. All the masters whom I have met have lives that follow this pattern. They have told me it would be impossible for them to change it, since in it lies the secret of their physical vitality and the knowledge of their art. "The recipe is good since it has been practiced for hundreds of years," P. S. Balachandran assures me with a smile.

INTERVIEWS WITH TWO MASTERS

I conducted interviews with two great Kalaripayat masters, one of whom practices southern style and the other northern style. P. S. Balachandran teaches at the Indian School of Martial Art (Trivandrum) and Sathya Narayanan teaches at C. V. N. Kalari

(Trivandrum). These two individuals are completely different from each other, but they are united in their efforts to defend their art and preserve their tradition.

India is one of the foremost film producers in the world and Indian producers have become interested in Kalaripayat for the violence and the spectacle that it can add to the impact of their films. Scenarios have already been concocted in studios in Mumbai and Chennai, and it's very likely that in the coming years Kalaripayat will enjoy a lucrative flowering through cinema entertainment.

Patrick Denaud: Your ancestors, the Nair warriors, practiced Kalaripayat in order to wage war. What about you?

P. S. Balachandran: Kalaripayat is not only about the art of war, but also helps to improve character so we can become more human. It encourages respect for tradition and it allows us to use peace as a weapon if we are attacked. Physically and psychically I feel strong, which is really necessary at this point in time. Of course sometimes it is necessary to fight but only if it's a question of life or death; we must never fight from hatred. Our history tells us that Kalaripayat was created by the gods to give man a warrior's stance in confronting life, a warrior who does not take his orders from men but from the gods and from love. There is but one God who is omnipresent; there is but one religion, the religion of love; there is but one caste, the caste of humanity; there is but one language, the language of the heart. This too is taught by Kalaripayat.

Sathya Narayanan: Kalaripayat is the heritage I received from my grandparents so I have a duty to practice it and teach it. It's also good physical exercise that keeps me strong. If I'm attacked, I don't have to fight; besides I wouldn't know how to do so since my spiritual force would prevent me from fighting and I would naturally reason with the opponent. People are always trying to measure themselves against each other because they don't know themselves.

What I do is fight only with myself. The Westerner who wants to understand Kalaripayat will very likely be puzzled. He comes from another world, he was born into another civilization, and he is engaged in a different system of thought and a different way of life.

Patrick Denaud: It's said that some Kalaripayat masters train students in fighting when there is conflict between Hindu and Muslim communities.

P. S. Balachandran: If certain people do that, they are not Kalaripayat masters. In my classes there are Hindus, Muslims, and Christians; they live together like brothers and there is never any conflict. Kalaripayat teaches us to live in a brotherly way with others. It's obvious that Kalaripayat, an art that can be deadly, should not be taught to people who are fired up and who have no sense of values. The master must be discerning.

Sathya Narayanan: This has already happened in the north of the country when there have been Hindu-Muslim conflicts. Some people are using weapons that they have practiced with in the kalari, such as the kettukari, or stave, for example.

But it is not the masters who are behind this; they have been taken advantage of by their students; these students have not really studied and understood the Kalaripayat philosophy.

Patrick Denaud: What is the difference between Kalaripayat and other martial arts such as karate?

P. S. Balachandran: Often students choose karate to get quick results; in the practice of Kalaripayat you have to work a long time to reach a certain level. Perfection is important.

Kalaripayat is a complete art in which weapons practice and medical knowledge are possible only after long years of hard work and study. Because of this, Kalaripayat is not at present a commercial martial art.

People who do karate in India set aside its spiritual side and don't practice meditation. Perhaps in Japan it's different but not in India and I think that it's the same in Europe. Who is able to get up at 5 every morning to practice his art? Kalaripayat is essentially a form of renunciation, almost a sacred calling.

Sathya Narayanan: Karate is a sport, whereas in Kalaripayat there is no competition. It's also a way of inner development, a style of living. Many people think that Kalaripayat is a sport but after a few lessons they see that they were mistaken and they give it up. Of ten people who come to practice Kalaripayat, two months later there will only be two left.

People think Kalaripayat has secrets and they want to find them out. The only secret is renunciation and regularity in practice, so they are disappointed. The secret cannot be transmitted; it must be conquered. The master can only advise and encourage.

The best age to start Kalaripayat is between ten and fifteen; after that it's too late. In order to become very good at it, you need a minimum of ten years of practice.

Karate as it is practiced today lacks a spiritual dimension and we are probably very far from how it was taught by Japanese masters at the beginning of the twentieth century. Unfortunately, as Kalaripayat loses its values, it will one day come to resemble karate.

Patrick Denaud: What is the future of Kalaripayat?

P. S. Balachandran: Today Kalaripayat is not a financially cost-effective and profitable activity. Its teachers are poor. For example, master K. Velayadhan, who is almost blind, still, at the age of eighty, sees patients in order to make a living.

When a master agrees to teach a student, he must take the *gurudakshina* (money and gifts that a student offers the guru). This tradition of giving a dakshina is almost obligatory. The student has to decide on the amount. In spite of their hardships, masters out of modesty never ask for dakshina.

I survive because I'm given money for the medical treatments. I also ask for fees from those who sign up for my courses and I accept dakshina only once.

For Kalaripayat to continue to exist, the masters need to be able to live decently. We need to be able to continue to encourage its development among young people. I would like to see us find an Indian Bruce Lee to promote our Kalaripayat; then young people would come to do Kalaripayat. We need to teach our art to the world, but we must remain vigilant so that, as it is commercialized, it doesn't lose its values.

Sathya Narayanan: There really is no future in the short term, because there's no money to be made while at the same time much effort has to be expended. There are five hundred gurus in Kerala and 150 in the Trivandrum district; most of them are poor.

Certain members of the Kalaripayat association, for commercial reasons, want to give it a sports orientation but most masters do not agree. Kalaripayat is a martial art, not a sport. The profound message that underlies this legendary art must be understood. Today it is torn between tradition and modernity. It is in danger and our politicians need to preserve it and encourage it because it is our national heritage.

In our working together we also need to make it known to the international community while still preserving our traditions.

KALARIPAYAT PRACTITIONERS

In response to the question "Why do you practice Kalaripayat?" here is what some students had to say:

> *So I know how to defend myself and keep my body flexible. I also want to be strong and bolster my health. I saw demonstrations of Kalaripayat on television and it interested me.*
>
> P. S. PARABODH, AGE 12

> *Because it's good for my body, and because I want others to respect me in my everyday life. It is a way to be strong and to make peace prevail.*
>
> KRISSNA PRAVEEN, AGE 14

> *Kalaripayat helps self-control and also helps to overcome problems in life. It's the freedom to express myself through my body. When you begin with Kalaripayat the pleasure is muscular; muscles get discovered. Then, with time and practice, the pleasure is transformed and you feel something taking place inside.*
>
> CRONESH KUMAR T. K., AGE 16

> *Kalaripayat helps me to maintain the flexibility of my body, to feel good physically, and to control my emotions when I'm in difficult situations. It helps me keep a good moral attitude. It improves my decision-making and discrimination and makes me more effective in my day-to-day life.*
>
> RAVI BALAGOPAL, AGE 21

I want to become a Kalaripayat master, someone who
teaches others peace.

V. R. VIVEK, AGE 12

My ancestors practiced Kalaripayat and I continue
the tradition since I think that it's good for my body
and my mind. It helps me build an identity. For me,
Kalaripayat has allowed me to become aware of how
fear operates. I have learned to reason with myself and
overcome my emotions.

GIRISH KUMAR, AGE 18

7

The Influence of India on Asia and of Kalaripayat on the Martial Arts

India either frightens or fascinates. Either you detest her or she charms you. You need to come to know her with restraint, humility and love. And if you succeed, what a shock! For the forty years that I have traveled throughout India, I never cease to be enchanted:

By its people, its scenery, and its everyday life, the legendary heritage of a past that is one of the oldest and richest in the world;

By a vitality that demonstrates moment by moment that, although adversity is great, man knows how to be greater than adversity;

By an innate sense of beauty that transforms the poorest peasant woman walking to the well with her copper pitcher on her head into the statue of a temple goddess;

*By a taste for the sacred which means that god appears
more often and in more places than anywhere else.*

DOMINIQUE LAPIERRE

The carefully established and highly developed disciplines of combat and meditation of India and China are well-ordered and precise systems that are not to be found elaborated to the same degree elsewhere during the Christian era. Did they arise independently in these two worlds or did one of them pass on its secrets to the other? Answers to this question can be found in Indian historic and cultural sources from eras that predate the spread of Buddhism to the Far East.

INDIA'S NOBLE ART OF WAR

In India's Brahmanic era (prior to 500 BCE), combat techniques and the art of war were always considered as a noble art that would lead to purity of body and mind, to a strengthening of the physique that would allow the athlete to attain the aims of an existence sanctioned by Brahmanism. Martial arts techniques are to be found in all the great sacred books of India. We find them, for example, in the two famous epic poems, the Mahabharata and the Ramayana*: these two books include very many combat scenes in which the heroes use their divine talents to engage and vanquish their enemies in battle. The meditation techniques that ensure their invincibility in combat are also largely described (see figure 7.2).

The *Manava Dharmasastra,* literally "the book of the law of

---

*"Rama's Journey," a great epic poem written in a relatively commonplace form of Sanskrit by a man named Valmiki who lived at the beginning of our era. This long text has a great deal to teach us about the code of conduct in India during this era and also about the psychology of the upper castes at that time.

Fig. 7.2. Illustration of battle scene in the Ramayana.

Manu," is an ancient work drawn up in the south of India. It determines the appropriate conduct in various periods of a person's existence and contains religious duties, purifications, political concepts, and military arts. The name of Manu is applied to each of seven divine personages who, according to Indian thinking, successively governed the world. It is said that "the book of the law" was revealed by the god Brahma himself to the first Manu named Swayambhuva. The following excerpt is from book seven.

> Never flee from combat, protect the common folk, revere the Brahmins, these are the principal duties that will bring felicity to the kings who carry them out. When sovereigns who want to conquer one another during battles fight with great courage and without turning away their heads, such sovereigns go directly to heaven when they die.

In an engagement with an enemy, a warrior must never use evil weapons such as sticks studded with nails, barbed arrows, poisoned arrows or flaming shafts.*

He must not strike an enemy who is on foot when he is riding a chariot himself, nor must he strike an effeminate man, nor a man who is praying for mercy, nor a man whose hair is undone, nor one who is seated, nor one who says, "I am your prisoner," nor a man asleep, nor one who has no armor, nor one who is naked, nor one who has been disarmed, nor one who is watching the battle but is not taking part in it, nor one who is already fighting someone else, nor one whose weapon is broken, nor one who is overcome with sorrow, nor a man who is seriously wounded, nor a coward, nor a retreating soldier. A brave warrior must remember his duties.

The coward who takes flight during combat and who is killed by his enemies, takes on all the bad actions of his leader, whatever they may be; and if the deserter who is killed has stored up some good actions for another life, it's his leader who will repeat all the benefit of them.

May his troops be constantly engaged, may his true worth come forth, may he hide carefully what has to be kept secret, may he always watch out for the enemy's weak points.

The king whose army is constantly engaged is feared by everyone; consequently, may he ensure that his military forces respect the populace.

Like the heron, may he reflect on the advantages that he might obtain; like the lion, may his true worth come forth; like the

---

*It is thought that what is being spoken of here are rockets loaded with an inflammable mixture similar to that of Greek fire (burning liquid) or cannon powder, but it is not at all certain. The flaming shafts mentioned in the text of Manu may simply have been arrows loaded with inflammable materials. Similar things were used in ancient times.

wolf, may he attack unexpectedly; like the hare, may he conduct his retreat with caution.

The wise consider an invincible enemy to be one who is educated, of noble extraction, brave, clever, generous, full of gratitude for those who have helped him, and unshakable in his intention.

Goodness, the art of knowing men, worth, compassion, and inexhaustible generosity: such are the virtues that adorn a fair-minded prince.

BUDDHA: MARTIAL ART ADEPT

While for the Buddha, the struggle and the different forms of combat could have no other meaning than a spiritual one, before his awakening (the extinction of desire) he was trained in fencing, archery, and unarmed combat: skills of the sword-wielding nobility to which he belonged. The *Lalitavistara*—a composition in Sanskrit prose and verse from between the second century BCE and the second century CE—details the early life of the Buddha, as related by him to his disciples. This text was translated into Chinese by Dharmaraksha around the year 308.

The *Lalitavistara* refers to the Buddha as the Bodhisattva* and presents him displaying his prowess in martial arts with the other young men of the Cakya court. His participation in this tournament of sporting activities seems to be the culmination of military and athletic training appropriate to a king's son. It should be noted that the *Lalitavistara* also mentions his mastery in striking pressure points.

It is interesting and illuminating to review a few passages from the *Lalitavistara:*

---

*"Enlightened Being," the name given to Buddhism's saintly personages; in this case it refers to the Buddha himself.

And the son of the gods who reside in the vastness of Heaven above gave voice to these *gathas:**

> *During kotis*† *and during kalpas,*§ *through the merit gained from devotion and austerity, through self-denial, through strength of patience and through power over oneself, if this is how he has turned his body and mind to lightness, learn just to what extent he excels in alacrity.*

> *You know nothing of his departure and of his return so great is the supernatural power that he has attained. Who then here could produce this miraculous speed? He is unequaled. Be respectful of him.*

> *By performing these kinds of feats the Bodhisattva distinguishes himself by his superiority.*

Then the Cakyas say: "We want the young man to show his superiority also in fighting."

Then the Bodhisattva stood all alone on one side and the five hundred Cakyas, having assembled, stood ready to fight on their side. Nanda and Ananda,** both having approached the Bodhisattva planning to do battle with him, were however not even touched by his hand but instead, unable to withstand his force and his splendor, tumbled backward to the ground.

Immediately following this, the young Cakya Devadatta,† proud and swelling with arrogance from his strength and from being one of the Cakyas, ventured forth against the Bodhisattva, making a circuit of the arena and then pouncing on him. Then

---

*Lyric verses intended to be sung in Buddhist texts.

†A unit of measure equal to ten million.

§Represents the total duration of the creation of a universe, meaning about 4,320,000,000 of our years.

**Ananda was the half brother and cousin of the Buddha.

†This is the Buddha's cousin who, out of jealousy, tried to kill him.

the Bodhisattva, untroubled and unhurried, having gently taken the young Devadatta in his right hand, and, with no thought of harming him but only wanting to diminish his arrogance, out of his goodness, made him spin around three times in the air and then set him down without harming his body.

Next he said, "Enough, enough of this fighting! Come, all of you, all at once and fight."

And all together, carried away by arrogance, they attacked the Bodhisattva. But they were not even touched and, unable to withstand the nobility, the majesty, and the strength of his body, they immediately fell backward to the ground.

At this moment, gods and men by the hundreds of thousands shouted out great cries of admiration; and the sons of the gods, who stood by in the great expanse of the heavens sent down a shower of flowers and recited in chorus these gathas:

> *All the beings that exist in the ten points of space, if*
> *they were like a single fearsome fighter, they would be*
> *overturned in a moment; as soon as they would be touched*
> *by the most eminent of men, they would be thrown*
> *backward to the ground.*
>
> *Mount Meru* and Sumeru as well as the Chakravala*
> *universe, and as well as any other mountains, throughout*
> *the ten points of space, by touching them with his hands, he*
> *would turn them to dust. What a marvel is he who, in a*
> *human body, is without materiality!*
>
> *Those who, having become masters of their body, have*
> *truly conquered their body's limitations; those who, being*
> *masters of their words, speak always in a reserved way;*

---

*Mythic mountain said to be the axis of the world, Meru represents for yogis the spinal column.

those who, having subdued their senses, are calm and have a
tranquil mind, why would such people veil their faces?

It was in doing such things that the Bodhisattva distinguished himself by his superiority.

Then Dandapani addressed the following words to the young Cakyas: "Having seen what you wanted to see, engage now in the art of archery."

Right away, Ananda set an iron drum as a target at a distance of two *kroshas*;* after him, Devadatta set an iron drum as a target at a distance of four kroshas; after him, Sundarananda set an iron drum as a target at a distance of six kroshas; after him, the Cakya Dandapani set an iron drum as a target at a distance of two *yojanas.*†

Then the Bodhisattva, after having set an iron drum as a target at a distance of ten kroshas, arranged seven *talas* trees beside it and, after that, an iron warpiece with a boar's face.

Then Ananda hit the drum placed as a target at a distance of two kroshas, but he could not do better. Devadatta hit the drum placed as a target at a distance of four kroshas, without being able to do better. Sundarananda hit the drum placed as a target at a distance of six kroshas, without being able to do better. Dandapani hit the drum placed as a target at a distance of two yojanas, and his arrow went right through it but he was unable to do better. Then the Bodhisattva, having broken one by one all the bows he'd been given, said, "Is there in the city, some other bow which, when I draw it will withstand the force of my body and support my effort?"

The king [father of the Bodhisattva] said, "Yes, my son there is

---

*Name given to an ancient measure of distance equal to about 2.2 miles.
†An ancient measure of distance equal to four kroshas (about 9 or 10 miles).

one." The young man asked, "Sire, where is it?" The king replied, "Your grandfather Sinhahanu (lion's jawbone) had a bow, which is now honored in the temple of the gods with perfumes and garlands, and no one, up to now, has been able to lift it."

The Bodhisattva said, "Sire, have this bow brought and we will try it." The bow was then immediately brought, and none of the young Cakyas, no matter how hard they tried, were able to lift this bow, nor therefore could anyone draw it.

Then the bow was presented to the Cakya Dandapani, and even though he tried as hard as he could, he was able to lift the bow but not draw it.

The bow was then presented to the Bodhisattva; and he, having seized the bow without getting up from his seat, sitting with his legs half crossed, held it in left hand and drew it with one finger of his right hand.

At the moment when this bow was drawn in this way, the sound echoed throughout the great city of Kapilavastu and all its inhabitants, frightened, asked each other what this noise could be. Then they were told that the young Sarvathasiddha had drawn his grandfather's bow and the sound had come from that.

Then gods and men by the hundreds of thousands began to shout out cries of astonishment and admiration, and the sons of the gods, who stood by in the great expanse of the heavens addressed this gatha to King Suddhodana and to the great multitude of people:

> *Since this bow was drawn by the Muni without even getting up from his seat and without making any effort, there is no doubt that the Muni will soon have accomplished his plans after he has vanquished the army of Mara.**

---

*The prince of demons who tried to tempt the Buddha while he was meditating under the Bo Tree.

So then, reverently, having drawn the bow and having taken an arrow, the Bodhisattva let it fly with the same force. And passing through the drum of Ananda, the drum of Devadatta, the drum of Sundarananda, the drum of Dandapani, passing through them all, the arrow pierced, at a distance of ten kroshas, the iron drum that he himself had placed as a target. It then went through the seven *talas* trees, and finally went right through the warpiece having a face of a boar; continuing on, it struck into the earth and disappeared. At the spot where this arrow pierced the soil and entered the earth, a well was formed which still today is called Carakupa, or "the well of the arrow."

At this same moment, the gods and men by the hundreds of thousands shouted out great cries of astonishment and admiration, and the entire assembly of Cakyas in wonder said to each other, "It's a marvel in truth! Without having studied, he has such skill in the arts!"

And the sons of the gods who stood by in the great expanse of the heavens spoke as follows to King Suddhodana and to the great multitude of people, "Why such great astonishment and what is its cause?"

After having spoken in this way, the sons of the gods showered the *Bodhisattva* with a profusion of flowers and went on their way.

And the same it was, in jumping, in the science of writing, of seals, of calculation, of arithmetic, of wrestling, and of archery; in running and swimming, in the art of letting arrows fly, of driving an elephant by mounting on its neck, or a horse by mounting on its back; in the art of driving chariots, in the practice of archery; for steadfastness, strength, and courage; in the arm action required in driving an elephant with a hook, in the action of getting up, going out, going down; in tying fists, tying feet, and tying locks of hair; in the action of cutting, splitting, traversing, shaking, or piercing what is not set going, of piercing the joint, of piercing what resonates, in the action of striking hard . . .

The Bodhisattva, surpassing the work of gods and men, alone is eminently distinguished by his superiority . . .

It was this tradition of Hindu martial arts and other fields of knowledge that traveled to China.

THE SPREAD OF BRAHMANISM TO CHINA

A careful analysis of historical accounts shows the possible transmission into China of certain Brahmanic ideas and practices in the first millennium of our era and earlier. Lao-tzu, who visited western India, was the founder of the widespread Far Eastern religion of Taoism, from the Chinese *tao,* meaning "reason or supreme being." He wrote his *Tao Te Ching* in 550 BCE. This five-thousand-word teaching on moral conduct that leads to the Tao has many similarities to the Indian Brahmanic texts of the *Upanishads* (texts that provide explanations of the universe) and especially to the *Bhagavad Gita* (India's Bible) in which Krishna teaches the art of yoga in songs 3 to 6.

In Central Asia, on the trade routes from India to China, along which Buddhism's great expansion took place, a great many texts that are without religious character have been discovered along with Buddhist texts. The fact that Buddhists carried such texts proves that Indian teachings other than those in the sacred books could have spread to the Far East.

The bibliographic catalog of the official history of the Sui Dynasty that Wei Zeng completed in 610 CE contains the titles of many works now lost, which begin with the syllables *po lo men,* meaning "Brahmin." Among them are to be found *Polomen Tianwen Jing* (Brahmin astronomy), *Polomen Suanfa* (Brahmin mathematics),

Polomen Yinyang Suan Jing (Brahmin method of time calculation), *Polomen Yao Fang* (Brahmin drugs and prescriptions).

Duan Chengshi wrote in 780 in his *Yoyang zazu*:

> Wang Xuanrong captured an Indian prince named Geluo Shushun. He had with him a scholar versed in unusual arts who was called Naluo Misuobo who said he had the power to extend people's lives to two hundred years. The emperor Tai Zong was astounded and invited him to come to live at Jin Yan Men palace and manufacture remedies that were to prolong life. . . . The Indian scholar said that in his country there was a substance called "water of Ban Cha Zhuo," that was extracted from mountain minerals. There were seven kinds of this water with different colors. It was sometimes hot and sometimes cold. It was capable of dissolving plants, wood, metals, and iron. Any hand that touched it would be destroyed.

Some manuscript texts found recently in Chinese Turkistan are fragments of a book on black magic written in Sanskrit. The magic spells found in this book contain many names of gods belonging only to Hinduism and not to Buddhism. The dating of this manuscript is that of China's Tang dynasty: 618–907. This is the period that tantric books—practical manuals of Buddhist and Hindu esotericism—began to be introduced into China. They are filled with instructions for symbolic or magic rituals, they illustrate and promote fantastic pantheons of gods, and they teach how to practice mental states as well as physical and psychic exercises from yoga.

The content of these books is borrowed in part from Hinduism in general and particularly from the ancient texts known as the *puranas* (literally, "ancient times"): ancient traditional texts in Sanskrit, the sacred language of Brahmanism, dealing with a wide range of subjects such as the creation of the world, the genealogies of mystical sovereigns, mythologies, castes, and so on. Sometimes the Tantras remain purely Hindu, while sometimes they take on a strongly Buddhist coloring; it's in their Buddhist forms that they frequently appear in China.

These ideas traveled not only through the trade routes of Central Asia but also across the seas. In the eighth century, Chinese vessels plied the southern oceans and the Persian Gulf, mooring in Kerala at the port now called Kollam. In the same region in the Vijayanagara era (a Hindu dynasty and empire founded in 1336), wall paintings showing both Arab and Chinese figures bear witness to a flourishing commerce along this ancient maritime trade route.

All these influences that spread beyond the borders of India were everywhere facilitated through translations from Sanskrit literature, which was for India what Latin was for Europe—a means of unifying the culture at large and an instrument for the diffusion of ideas.

CHINESE YOGA: TAI CHI CHUAN

It is justified to assume that the Taoists borrowed Indian theories of vital energy and breathing exercises, because India is known to have elaborated these theories and techniques in the first part of the millennium before Christ, an era preceding these developments in China. Additionally, the use of Indian words in Taoism's present-day technical terminology is proof of a definite Indian influence.

The practice of tai chi chuan, the bare-hands art of self-defense, is characterized by a unique set of gymnastics that were codified and documented. We find that they are all designed to take place within a circle, the circle being a representation of mind-body equilibrium and harmony. Dating from the Tang era (618–907), this codified repertoire of Chinese gymnastic movements, still studied today, does mention Indian gymnastic exercises. *One Thousand Medical Recipes or Precious*

Prescriptions by the famous Sun Simiao* includes a chapter titled "Nourishing the Body with Vital Breath" and a sub-chapter titled "Brahmanic Procedure or Massage from the Country of India." In this chapter numerous martial gymnastic movements are described as well as a method to control breathing and some techniques of massage from the south of India. He describes a method of breathing control used in medicine and in the practice of tai chi chuan that is divided into five sections: 1) breathing out, 2) shouting and uttering cries, 3) breathing in, 4) breathing out slowly, 5) blowing the breath out.

Several exercises are also mentioned such as the *laoniu biqi*, or "breathing deeply like an old steer." These breathing exercises are what constitute "standing gymnastics," or *qigong*. They are designed to produce a "quiet breathing," or *fanxi*.

These examples seem to confirm the Indian influence on tai chi chuan, which is sometimes called "Chinese yoga." The *Qian jin fang* had a significant influence in China but also in Japan where it became a study manual. Tanbu Yasuyori, official doctor at the Japanese court, was very influenced by this book when he wrote the *Ishinpo* in 982. The *Ishinpo* includes procedures specific to Indian massage as well as gymnastic movements that originated in India.

BODHIDHARMA OR DA MO

When the eagle attacks, he dives without extending his wings. When the tiger is on the point of leaping on his prey, he crawls with his ears flattened back. In the same way, when a sage is about to act no one can guess it.

---

*Sun Simiao (581–682) also compiled the oldest treatise on ophthalmology and is often called the King of Remedies.

One of the most famous transmitters of Buddhist teachings to China was Bodhidharma or Da Mo (ca. 470–549?), who is referred to by certain palm leaf manuscripts from the twelfth century. According to legend, he was the third son of Sughanda, sovereign of the kingdom of Tamil Nadu at Kanchipuram in the south of India. Having been educated in the most strict warrior tradition, the prince was initiated into Kalaripayat at an early age.

He was also the student of the Buddhist master Prajnatara. Buddhism advocated giving up the ego and its desires—the source of pain.* So, donning the cloak of a wandering monk, Da Mo gave up wealth and power in order to teach Buddhist doctrine, to advance his own studies, and to achieve enlightenment. Intensive meditation was an essential element of his research.

Da Mo practiced a form of meditation that was designed to focus his mind on a point. Achieving this inner area of concentration is comparable to one of the principles of the martial arts: moving your physical force and your energy toward a vulnerable pressure point on the adversary's body. This work in meditation removes from the psyche all feelings of passion, a condition that is essential for reaching full concentration.

In order to obtain liberation and enlightenment, Da Mo remained in a cave, facing a wall, for nine years. He meditated while listening to the sound of ants; this technique of wall watching, combined with optimal attitudes, supported the prolonged cessation of all movement and all sensation. Legend has it that, to prevent his meditation from being interrupted by sleep, Da Mo tore off his eyelids. On the ground where they fell sprang up the shrub from which we now harvest tea.

Da Mo thus discovered a way of nondoing that leads to peace and longevity. Out of this Chan Buddhism emerged, as well as the

---

*Having arisen out of Brahmanism, Buddhist doctrine is in fact simply a kind of Protestantism that, without contradicting the traditional teachings or gods, prefers to put its accent on the causes of human suffering and the means of overcoming it.

technique of meditation that later was to become Zen, which would conquer Japan, arriving there by way of Okinawa.

After having attained enlightenment, and upon the death of his mentor, Da Mo decided to travel to China on foot in order to preach the Buddha's teaching. According to tradition he took with him the begging bowl that had been used by the Buddha. After a long and difficult voyage, Da Mo arrived at the court of Emperor Wu of Liang (464–549).

Following a period of disagreement over Buddhist doctrine, Da Mo was sent into exile from the court. He walked for a long time toward the north and finally arrived at the Buddhist monastery of Shaolin, the "little forest" temple that had been founded, according to tradition, in 496 on Mount Song in Henan. Da Mo found that most of the monks were in poor physical health. He therefore introduced them to a series of exercises based on meditation and breathing techniques. Twelve daily exercises were introduced into Shaolin practice in this way, exercises which, by the way, are still practiced by monks in Nepal. These exercises are found in the *Yi Jin Jing*, a manual for exercising the muscles and tendons written by Da Mo. Briefly described, they are:

1. The body erect, arms folded on the chest. The breath is mastered and the spirits are controlled. Heart-Mind is calm.
2. Standing on tiptoe, arms outstretched horizontally. Heart-Mind quiet. The breath is calmed. Looking fixedly.
3. Hands joined above the head as if holding up the sky.
4. The right arm raised toward the sky with the palm turned toward the head as if directed at the two pupils. Breathing through the nose is harmonized gradually. The exercise alternates between right and left.
5. An exercise of strength intended to activate the circulation of breath on both left and right sides; one fist after the other is turned toward the two pupils.

6. The arms, extended forward, are brought back with energy to their initial position.

7. The left arm is moved behind the nape of the neck and the hand comes right to the face. The right arm is similarly moved behind the back. The body is upright; the breath is calm. Carefully follow the rotation left, then right.

8. With the hand outstretched well, the position consists of crouching down to the ground with the legs.

9. The position called the "dragon studying his claws" involves rotation of the shoulders.

10. The posture of the "tiger hunting his food" suggests a position on all fours, with an animal gait.

11. The hands are cupped behind the neck. The body is bent toward the ground.

12. The body is completely bent toward the ground but the head is held up and the hands are brought together and touch the ground.

Da Mo brought several texts with him from India, notably those dealing with martial arts and with Kalaripayat. Using them, he introduced the combat art practiced in the south of India at Shaolin. Subsequently, Da Mo developed these techniques into complete systems of combat and self-defense. Shaolin boxing, the starting point of all the great martial arts of Asia, took its first steps in just this way. These systems were kept secret and were taught only to those among the monks who were in full-time residence at the monastery. At this stage, the combat techniques were not intended for the purposes of aggression but were meant instead to provide a means of controlling the body and the mind.

The palm leaf manuscripts indicate that Da Mo later returned to India, where he died as a hermit around the year 550 CE.

Nearly fourteen centuries after the arrival of Da Mo, Shaolin

Monastery retains its legendary aura. In the courtyard and training rooms of the monastery, the battered paving stones indicate how harsh the training was. From generation to generation the monks passed on the spirit of Da Mo's teaching, in which purification of the mind and disciplining of the body went hand in hand. Only when the body is strong enough to be able to resist the temptations of the external world can the heart and mind find peace and truth. Regardless of his strength and his combat qualities, the first adversary of a disciple of Da Mo will always be his own self.

Later, government persecution and the burning down of the Shaolin Monastery scattered the monks. During this period the carrying of arms was forbidden by the government; the monks trained at Shaolin felt that it was their duty to teach combat arts to the oppressed masses to help them protect themselves against bandits and against the corrupt regime. The art of combat began to spread among the populace in various parts of China, then into other countries.

When Zen Buddhism made its way to Japan with its martial arts component, it stopped over in Okinawa, where Kalaripayat fused with local combat techniques to become karate. Outside of the contribution of certain Kalaripayat techniques by the Bodhidarma at Shaolin, the ancient combat and yogic techniques of India have certainly contributed the most to martial arts as they are practiced today. If India's influence has not been decisive, it has certainly been significant. Today both Japan and China are beginning to look to India to rediscover the origin of all the great martial arts of Asia.

Where to Practice

IN INDIA

Indian School of Martial Arts
Trivandrum
Kerala
India
Phone: +91 471 64140

C. V. N. Kalari
Trivandrum
Kerala
India
Phone: +91 471 74182

IN FRANCE

Cécile Gordon was the first European practitioner to specialize in the art of Kalaripayat. She founded the C. V. N. Kalari association, which organizes lectures, courses, and trips relating to Kalaripayat:

Association Kalaripayat C. V. N. Kalari
Rouze d'Ustou
09140 Seix

Glossary

Agastya Maharshi: A great sage and legendary master of Kalaripayat.

Agni Purana: A traditional Sanskrit text dealing with various subjects such as the creation of the world, legends, and mythologies, composed in an encyclopedic form of twelve thousand stanzas.

Ankathari: Third phase of Kalaripayat training; combat exercises with weapons made from unbending metal.

Ayurveda: Traditional Indian medicine.

Bhagavati: "She who is blessed," one of the many names given to the goddess Shakti (energy).

Bodhisattva: "Enlightened Being," the name given to Buddhism's saintly personages, including at times the Buddha himself.

Brahma: Foremost god of the Hindu trinity, he is the lord of heaven and master of the horizon.

Brahmin: Member of the priestly class, the highest of India's traditional classes, charged with the integration of all formal acts of civilian life with religious rites and duties.

Buddhism: Having arisen out of Brahmanism, Buddhist doctrine is in fact simply a kind of Protestantism that, without contradicting the traditional teachings or gods, prefers to put its accent on the causes of human suffering and the means of overcoming it.

Cheruvati: A solid, heavy stick, fairly short, made of a kind of bamboo; one of the weapons of Kalaripayat.

Drona: A Brahmin who specialized in military science, one of the heroes of the Mahabharata.

Durga: Numerous temples are dedicated to this goddess or bear her name. She is a fearsome goddess who is usually shown riding on a lion or a tiger and is known for fighting demons.

Ganesha: The elephant-headed Hindu god, the son of Shiva and Parvati; he is the one who removes obstacles—based on this quality he has become a god of travelers.

Gathas: Lyric verses meant to be sung in Buddhist texts.

Guru: A guru is a guide who helps his disciples get rid of mental and emotional veils or screens that separate them from reality, allowing them to become aware of their oneness with ultimate reality.

Gurukkal: A Kalaripayat guru.

Jogo Do Pan: Portuguese wrestling sport that resembles Kalaripayat in its sequence of moves.

Kalari: The area with a surface of packed earth where Kalaripayat practice takes place. It is derived from the Sanskrit term *khalutika,* which means "a military training ground."

Kalarichikitsa: A form of Indian traditional medicine particular to Kalaripayat; a system of treatment specializing in orthopedic injuries and nervous disorders.

Kali: Goddess representing the destructive power of time.

Kalpa: Represents the total duration of the creation of a universe, meaning about 4,320,000,000 of our years.

Kamalashila: Buddhist priest who went to Tibet in 749 to found a monastery; he wrote numerous books on Buddhist doctrine.

Karma: In Hindu and Buddhist philosophy *karma* is the law of action that determines how each action or thought produces its effects on the spiritual totality of the being, and therefore influences his cosmic becoming, as well as determining his future incarnations.

Kattaram: A metallic weapon that is a kind of dagger used in combat duels fought at close range; one of the weapons of Kalaripayat.

Kettukari: Stave; a simple bamboo pole, thin and very long (about six feet); one of the weapons of Kalaripayat.

Kolthari: The second stage of Kalaripayat training, using wooden weapons.

Kotis: Unit of measure equal to ten million.

Krishna: The most venerated god in India. He is said to be the human incarnation of Vishnu in the third age of the world. He also symbolizes divine love, since he is the one who attracts.

Kroshas: An ancient measure of distance equal to about 2.2 miles.

Kshatriyas: Hindu warrior caste.

Mahabharata: One of the two greatest epic poems of India that has had an enormous influence on the thought, customs, festivals, and literature of India and of countries with an Indian civilization.

Mantra: A sacred Hindu or Buddhist formulation that distills into a material form the deity that it is intended to evoke. Mantras arose for the most part from the sacred syllable "OM."

Mantramukta: In traditional India, weapons thrown by machines.

Marman: Vital pressure points of the body indicating major concentrations of veins or nerves as well as tendons and the principal nerve plexuses.

Meithari: The first stage of Kalaripayat training; basic positions, jumps, and flexibility exercises to prepare the body.

Meru: Mythic mountain said to be the axis of the world; Meru represents for yogis the spinal column.

Mudra: Mystical gestures of the hands symbolizing the powers and mental attitudes of Hindu and Buddhist deities and spiritual masters.

Muktasandharita: In traditional India, weapons thrown and retrieved.

Nairs: The warrior caste indigenous to Kerala; the word *Nair* comes from *naga* in Sanskrit, meaning "serpent."

Nambudiris: Class of Brahmins originating in Malabar (southern Kerala); being very conservative, they still follow today certain rituals from the India's ancient texts.

Natya Shastra: Dance treatise in Sanskrit that assembles all knowledge about dance, music, and the art of theater.

Nirvana: Nirvana is the supreme state of non-existence, non-reincarnation, and of the integration of the being. It is not nothingness but rather the state of absolute purity that allows the soul to become integrated into the cosmos. In Buddhist philosophy it is more specifically represented as the extinction of the three passions: desire, hatred, and ignorance.

Ottakol: A specially designed curved wooden weapon of Kalaripayat.

Panimukta: In traditional India, weapons thrown by hand.

Paradevathai: One of the major gods of Kalaripayat, identified as a mixture of Shiva and Shakti, also identified with death and time, but with whom one can curry favor through propitiatory acts.

Parasurama: "Rama of the ax," legendary master of Kalaripayat; a courageous Brahmin, both wise and warlike, considered to be an incarnation of Vishnu.

Puranas: Ancient traditional texts in Sanskrit, the sacred language of Brahmanism, dealing with a wide range of subjects such as the creation of the world, the genealogies of mystical sovereigns, mythologies, castes, and so on.

Puttara: an altar installed in the western corner of a kalari.

Ragas: In classical Indian music, a blending of modes and rhythms intended to evoke a variety of sensations and emotions in the listener.

Raja: King, a title adopted by most Hindu chiefs who were landowners prior to Independence.

Rama: The solar incarnation of Vishnu, representing cosmic law. He brought happiness and peace during the second age.

Ramayana: "Rama's Journey," a great epic poem written in a relatively commonplace form of Sanskrit by a man named Valmiki who lived at the beginning of our era. This long text has a great deal to teach us about the code of conduct in India during this era and also about the psychology of the upper castes at that time.

Sanskrit: The classical language of India derived from ancient Indo-European languages that entered the valley of the Ganges with Western invaders. It is still the sacred language of Brahmanism.

Shakti: A Hindu goddess whose name means "energy."

Shaolin: Chinese Buddhist temple of the "little forest" founded, according to tradition, in Henan, on Mount Song in 496.

Shiva: One of the three major gods of the Brahmanic pantheon. He is considered as the destroyer.

Sushruta: Famous Indian doctor of the first century, to whom the composition of numerous ayurvedic medical treatises is attributed.

Tamil Nadu: State of the Indian union situated on the southwest coast of the Indian peninsula neighboring Kerala.

Tao: Reason or supreme being. In the practice of Chinese martial arts, *taos* are the basic movements.

Taoist: Widespread Far Eastern religion founded by Lao-tzu.

Urimi: A long and flexible sword, worn around the body like a belt; one of the weapons of Kalaripayat.

Uzhichil: A unique system of massage using the feet developed in Kalaripayat.

Viada: A heavy, two-handed club; one of the weapons of Kalaripayat.

Vishnu: One of the three major gods of the Hindu pantheon, who ensures the maintenance of the universe. He protects the moral and cosmic order when it is threatened and periodically descends to earth in a form that suits these purposes.

Yantramukta: In traditional India, weapons thrown by machines.

Yojana: An ancient measure of distance equal to four kroshas (about 9 or 10 miles).

Index

BOOKS OF RELATED INTEREST

The Spiritual Practices of the Ninja
Mastering the Four Gates to Freedom
by Ross Heaven

The Last Lama Warrior
The Secret Martial Art of Tibet
by Yogi Tchouzar Pa

Shaolin Qi Gong
Energy in Motion
by Shi Xinggui

Aikido and Words of Power
The Sacred Sounds of Kototama
by William Gleason

Martial Arts Teaching Tales of Power and Paradox
Freeing the Mind, Focusing Chi, and Mastering the Self
by Pascal Fauliot

Nei Kung
Taoist Techniques for Rejuvenating the Blood and Bone
by Mantak Chia

Iron Shirt Chi Kung
by Mantak Chia

Qigong Teachings of a Taoist Immortal
The Eight Essential Exercises of Master Li Ching-yun
by Stuart Alve Olson

INNER TRADITIONS • BEAR & COMPANY
P.O. Box 388
Rochester, VT 05767
1-800-246-8648
www.InnerTraditions.com

Or contact your local bookseller